GREEN THUMBS

GREEN THUMBS

A Kid's Activity Guide to Indoor and Outdoor Gardening

LAURIE CARLSON

CHICAGO REVIEW PRESS

Library of Congress Cataloging-in-Publication Data
Carlson, Laurie M., 1952–
    Green thumbs : a kid's activity guide to indoor and outdoor
gardening / Laurie Carlson — 1st ed.
        p. cm.
        Includes bibliographical references (p.   ) and Index.
        ISBN 1-55652-238-X : $12.95
        1. Gardening—Juvenile literature. 2. Nature craft—Juvenile
literature. 3. Handicraft—Juvenile literature. 4. Cookery—Juvenile
literature. [1. Gardening. 2. Nature craft. 3. Handicraft. 4. Cookery.]
I. Title.
SB457.C27 1995
635—dc20   94-41895
                                                                CIP
                                                                AC

The author and the publisher disclaim all liability incurred in
connection with the use of the information contained in this book.

Interior illustrations by Sean O'Neill
Typography by MobiGraphics, Inc., Chicago, Illinois

First edition
Published by Chicago Review Press, Incorporated
814 North Franklin Street
Chicago, Illinois 60610
ISBN 1-55652-238-X
Printed in the United States of America

5 4 3 2

"We can never have enough of nature."
—Thoreau

For my husband, Terry

Contents

INTRODUCTION

Welcome to the wonderful world of gardening! With a few seeds, some water, and soil, you'll be growing plants of your own in no time. As you enjoy the beauty of watching your plants grow a leaf at a time, you will learn about nature, about where living things come from. Gardening is a hobby that everyone in your family can take part in, and once you learn how to make things grow, it's an activity you can have fun with for the rest of your life.

An outdoor garden is a great way to get exercise and fresh air. You can be in the fresh air and imagine what it's like to live on a farm. This doesn't mean that you have to have a backyard to be a full-fledged gardener. If you have a windowsill with plenty of sunlight, you have most of what you need to start planting.

When you are the gardener, you can choose what you want to grow. Try growing some healthy food. No tomato from the grocery store is as tasty as the one that grew right before your eyes! Or you might want to plant flowers. It's fun to watch a little green sprout blossom into a colorful flower. You're the one who decides—you can do both.

Whether your garden is in a plot in the yard or a pot by a window, whether it's a bean plant or an African violet—you'll learn about how plants live and grow, and you'll enjoy some good things to eat and pretty flowers to gaze at.

By planting a garden, you'll discover many exciting things about nature right away: how the weather, temperature, and seasons affect all living things; how living things come out of seeds and soil; how the birds, earthworms, bees, and toads help in the garden; how our whole environment works together like an amazing puzzle.

So get up and get ready to plant. As budding gardeners, we're going to get in touch with the world we live in!

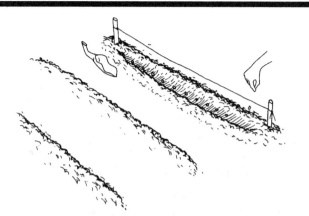

PLANTING BASICS

Plants need soil, water, sun, and air in order to live and grow. Minerals in the soil dissolve in water, and the plant roots suck them in; this is the plant's "food." The water travels up the plant stem and out to the leaves. In the leaves, the plant mixes this food with carbon dioxide. Carbon dioxide is in the air.

The plant leaves use the minerals and water from the soil and carbon dioxide from the air to grow. A special substance called *chlorophyll* (klor-oh-fill) is in the leaves. Chlorophyll and sunlight together make it all happen.

It's truly amazing what plants can do! The best part is that while the plant does all this mixing and growing, it gives off oxygen from its green leaves. Oxygen is what people and animals breathe, and it's very important for them to survive. You can see why we depend on plants!

Plants grow from seeds—even towering trees started from seeds. Each seed contains the beginning of a new plant and enough food to start its life. As the plant inside the seed grows, it pushes its way out of the seed. It needs air and water in order to do this.

As soon as the tiny plant gets roots, it needs more food than was stored inside the seed. Now it is ready to take food from the soil. It does this through tiny hairs that grow on the roots. The food in the soil dissolves in water and passes into the root hairs. From there, it moves from the roots up into the stem and out to all the parts of the plant.

How Plants Drink

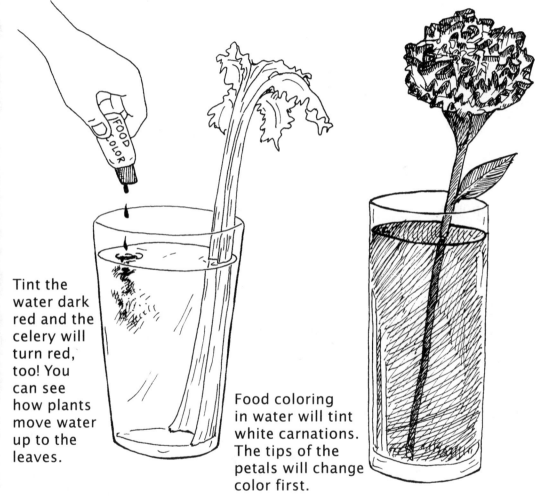

Tint the water dark red and the celery will turn red, too! You can see how plants move water up to the leaves.

Food coloring in water will tint white carnations. The tips of the petals will change color first.

Want to see how a plant sucks up water? This activity will show you.

MATERIALS

Celery or a white flower
Glass of water
Food coloring

Put several drops of red or blue food coloring in a glass of water. Put a piece of celery in the colored water. Within hours you can see the color begin to travel up the celery stem. The plant is pulling the water up to get it to the leaves. Try putting a white flower, such as a carnation, in colored water. Within a day, the color will have tinted the blossom.

Water for fields of broccoli in California travels in pipes from mountain lakes—up to 1,300 miles away!

Tool Time

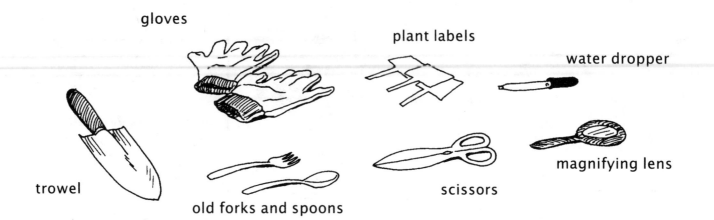

gloves

plant labels

water dropper

trowel

old forks and spoons

scissors

magnifying lens

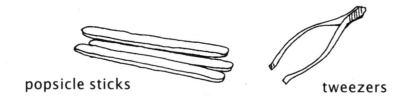

popsicle sticks

tweezers

You'll need some tools to work the soil, of course. You can save old forks, spoons, and kitchen scoops. Use a turkey baster to water hanging plants or delicate seedlings. Scissors are useful when you are taking cuttings or clipping away seedlings to thin a row. Look around and you may find lots of discarded items that can be useful in the garden. There are many tools and pieces of gardening equipment that you can make for yourself, too.

MATERIALS

Plastic milk jug

Scissors

Markers, decals, stickers, and other things to decorate with

Use scissors to cut away the top front section of a plastic milk jug. Decorate it with permanent markers, decals cut from adhesive-backed paper (like Contac), or stickers. Some useful things for outdoor gardeners are gloves, a trowel, old forks and spoons, scissors, plant labels and permanent markers to write on them with, and a ball of string for tying up plants that need support. Indoor gardeners need a tote to keep their special equipment in, too. Some things you will want to use for indoor plants are a water dropper, tweezers, a magnifying lens, popsicle sticks, and old forks and spoons.

You'll need something to carry your garden tools out to your work area.

Cut out and decorate a plastic jug. Fill it with your gardening tools.

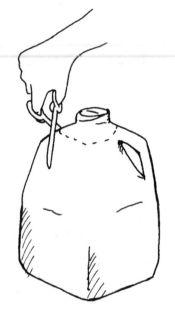

Punch holes in a plastic jug.

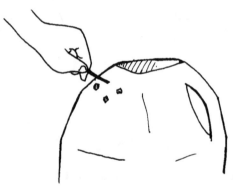

MATERIALS

Plastic milk jug
Scissors
Hole punch or large nail

Cut away the top part of a plastic milk jug with scissors. Punch holes in the front with a hole punch or large nail. Fill it with water and try pouring out some water to test it. Add more holes if the water pours out too slowly.

Plants need plenty of water. When the soil seems dry, water it thoroughly. Use enough water to wet the roots that are deep in the soil. Stop watering when the soil is evenly wet. Never let so much water into the garden or plant pot that it stands on the surface; you'll drown the plant! Here's an easy activity for making your own watering can.

MATERIALS

Plastic milk jug
Scissors

 Cut around the handle of a plastic milk jug. You can make scoops in several sizes to fit your different needs. Keep a large one at the compost pile, another at the potting bench, and a small one for digging little trenches for planting seeds.

Make simple scoops to use indoors or out.

One of the earliest gardens that people wrote about was the Garden of Eden. Some people think that it was located in the country we now know as Iraq.

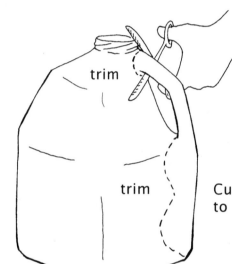

trim

trim

Cut around the handle to make a scoop.

Cut a plastic 1-liter pop bottle to make a scoop.

Use your scoop to dig and plant.

Make Straight Rows

When you're making an outdoor garden, you want the rows to be nice and straight. Here's a simple way to do that.

MATERIALS

Cord
Sticks

Cut a piece of cord a little longer than the length you want the plant row to be. Knot each end to a stick. Push one stick into the ground at one end of the row, and then take the other stick with you to the opposite end. Line up the sticks so that the cord runs straight, right where you want it. As you dig a trench and plant seeds, follow the cord and your row will be straight. Move the sticks and cord from row to row, as you work across the garden.

Make straight rows with sticks and cord.

MATERIALS

Plastic bottle
Permanent markers
OR
Aluminum pan
Old scissors
Ballpoint pen
Cardboard or Styrofoam
Popsicle stick and a hot-glue gun (with grown-up help), or thin wire and a hole punch

Plants have special names, and with so many growing things you may forget who's who. Make labels so that you will always remember.

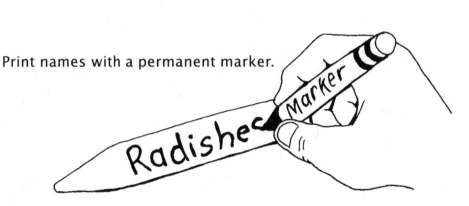

Print names with a permanent marker.

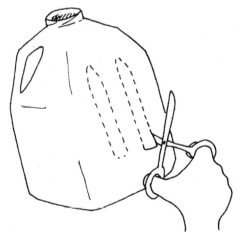

Cut strips from plastic bottles.

❀ Cut a strip from the side of a plastic bottle, and print the plant name with a permanent marker. Or you can use some old scissors (cutting metal makes new ones dull) to cut a piece from an aluminum pan, such as one from frozen foods. Use a ballpoint pen to write the name on the metal. Put a piece of soft cardboard or Styrofoam underneath as you write, so you won't accidentally tear the metal as you press on it. Print large, careful letters, and then use a hot-glue gun to attach the sign to a popsicle stick. Push it into the ground next to the growing plant. For trees and shrubs, punch holes in the ends of the sign and hang it from a branch with thin wire.

Cut pieces from aluminum pans.
Write on them with a ballpoint pen.

Use some cardboard as a cushion.

Glue to a stick or hang from a wire.

Plant Hats

Young seedlings need protection from the hot daytime sun or the cold evening temperatures.

MATERIALS

Plastic milk jug
Scissors

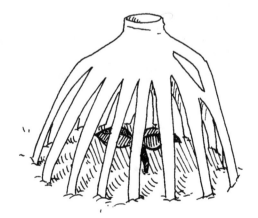 Cut away the bottom of a plastic milk jug, and then cut slits up the sides to make a simple cover for tiny seedlings that have just begun growing outdoors. Spread the slits apart and push the ends into the soil around the plant. When the seedlings are stronger, put the hats away for next year.

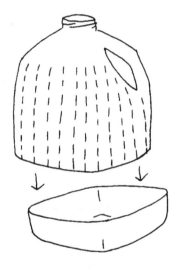

Cut off the base of a plastic jug.

Cut strips up the sides.

Position it in the soil to protect a new seedling.

MATERIALS

Pots

Potting soil

Broken pot pieces or aluminum foil

Pan or saucer

Ideas for seedling pots:
plastic milk jugs
plastic food containers
Styrofoam egg cartons
paper milk cartons

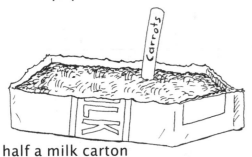

half a milk carton

Styrofoam egg cartons

You'll need to decide where to put your plants, whether in a windowsill or the backyard. Wherever you decide, make sure there is plenty of sunlight. You can bring water to the plants with a hose, a bucket, or a watering can (see page 8).

Indoor Gardens

You'll need pots and potting soil for indoor planting. You can purchase the soil in bags at garden centers. Lay a piece of a broken pot or crumpled aluminum foil over the hole in the bottom, so that the soil won't fall out. Put a layer of gravel in the bottom of the pot, then fill it with soil. Use a pan or saucer under the pot to catch water spills.

For indoor or patio planters, instead of buying pots, why not look around for things that will hold water and soil and let plant roots develop? Try using the bottoms of plastic milk jugs, milk cartons cut in half, cottage cheese containers, or even a basket lined with a heavy plastic bag.

To start seedlings you might want to save yogurt cups, Styrofoam egg cartons, and margarine tubs. Paper milk cartons cut in half lengthwise are good seed beds, too.

bottom of a plastic milk jug

Outdoor Gardens

For outdoor gardens, you'll need some tools to turn the soil and break it up: a shovel, rake, hoe, and trowel. You may want to wear gardening gloves and a sunhat. Remember to wear sunscreen whenever you work outside, even on cloudy days.

Look over the garden spot and make sure the soil is dry and flaky. If it's still wet from rain, let it dry out completely; if you don't, you'll only make hard clods that no plant's roots can break through. When you're ready to plant the garden, till the soil by lifting it and turning it with a shovel. Then, break up all the clods with a rake and hoe. Pick out any rocks or sticks.

Rake it smooth, and then use a trowel or your finger to carve a shallow trench to put the seeds in. Follow the directions on your seed packet. It will tell you exactly how far apart to put the seeds and how deep to cover them with soil. When you are finished, label the row with a plant label so that you'll know what's been planted while you're waiting for the tiny plants to appear.

MATERIALS

Shovel
Rake
Hoe
Trowel
Gardening gloves, sunhat, and sunscreen
Plant labels

Long ago, people planted crops when the moon was in a certain phase. They thought the plants would grow better, and some did. Scientists are still studying the moon's effect on plants.

The earliest garden plan is a map of an Egyptian garden drawn about 3,400 years ago. It had walkways and four ponds for ducks.

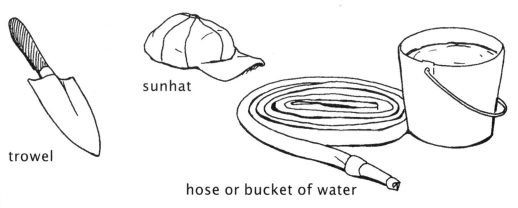

trowel

sunhat

hose or bucket of water

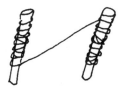

row markers

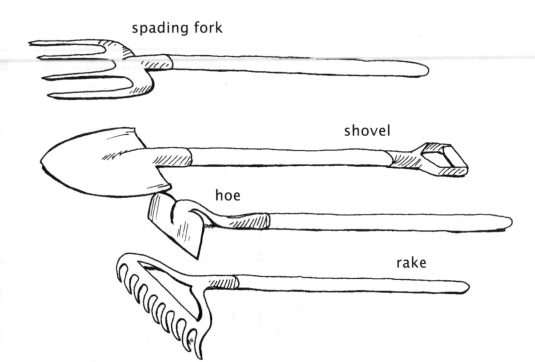

spading fork

shovel

hoe

rake

Topsoil *is the rich upper layer of soil where plants find the most nutrients. In the last hundred years, America's farmlands have lost half their topsoil. It washed into streams, rivers, and finally the ocean. In China, farmers have been farming without machinery and chemicals for four thousand years, with little loss of soil.*

digging stick

old spoon

plant labels

Create Some Compost

You have probably not given much thought to soil before, but now that you are a gardener, you will begin to think of it as much more than just *dirt*. Soil does more than hold up a plant so it can grow. It is filled with the minerals that a plant needs in order to be healthy and strong.

Not all soil is rich enough for good planting. Some is too full of rocks and gravel; some is too thick and sticky; and some soil is too full of mineral salts. Plants are like people, they need healthy meals to grow strong. You can enhance the soil you use in your garden to make it even more nutritious for your plants.

To make richer soil, we must put materials that were once living back into the soil. Things such as leaves, twigs, salad scraps, and grass clippings—all these will rot away as they put nutrients back into the soil. As plant materials rot away into the soil, they make a mixture that we call *compost*. It's loose, fluffy, and full of minerals plants love. As you work in your garden, be sure to set aside a spot for saving plant scraps, clippings, and leaves in a compost pile, where they can rot to make healthy soil to use in your garden and flower pots. When you see how much better plants grow in compost, you'll know why gardeners call it "Black Gold"!

Here are some things that are good to put in the compost pile:

Grass clippings
Leaves
Vegetable scraps
Fireplace ashes
Sawdust
Newspapers (torn into tiny pieces)
Weeds pulled from the garden
Twigs
Coffee grounds
Dryer lint
Peanut shells
Fruit peels

DO NOT USE: **pet droppings, meat scraps, colored newspapers, raw eggs, bones, butter or margarine, or other things that stink as they rot.**

Outdoor Compost Holder

Use a plastic laundry basket to make a compost holder. Ask an adult to help cut the bottom of the basket away, using a pair of heavy-duty scissors or a craft knife. Find a corner of the garden to dig a hole 6 inches deep in the shape of the bottom of the basket. Set the basket over the hole and fill it with a layer of compost material, about 4 inches deep. Sprinkle soil over the layer, then add another layer of compost material, then more soil. Layering will help the materials rot more quickly. If you think of the layers as going "brown (soil), green (compost material), brown, green . . . ," you won't forget.

Keep the compost heap wet, and turn things over once a week with a shovel to let air get to the bottom. When the material has rotted away, lift the basket and you'll find a layer of loose crumbly dark material at the bottom—compost. Add it to your garden or flower pots to make things grow better. Set up your compost holder again, and fill it for a fresh batch of compost.

MATERIALS

Plastic laundry basket

Heavy-duty scissors or craft knife (with grown-up help)

Soil

Compost materials (see list on page 17)

Lift it off the pile when the compost has rotted.

Cut the bottom out of a laundry basket.

Fill it with garden scraps.

MATERIALS

Large plastic box

Compost materials
(see list on page 17)

Soil

Earthworms
(from a fishing supply store)

Spray bottle

Scoop

Feed your garden the same kind of fertilizer American Indians used long ago. Indian farmers taught the Pilgrims to plant corn seeds in a hole with a dead fish. The fish enriched the soil as it rotted away, providing nutrients to help the plant grow. Today we don't need to plant a whole fish; we can buy plant food made of rotted fish that comes in plastic jugs. Your plants will love it!

Indoor Compost Holder

What if you can't compost outdoors? If it's winter, or you have no backyard, you can make a compost bin to keep indoors.

Use an old plastic picnic chest.

Use a large plastic box—an old picnic chest, the heavy plastic kind, works very well. Layer strips of shredded newspapers, vegetable scraps, and kitchen wastes, along with soil, in the box. Coffee grounds, vegetable peelings, and even dryer lint go in the box. Never use meat scraps or other things that will smell bad as they rot. Add a handful of earthworms. You can buy them at a fishing supply store. Keep the materials damp with a spray bottle, and stir with the scoop every few days. You'll start to see compost when the material turns dark and crumbly. You can use it in flower pots or add it to your garden soil outdoors.

Both vegetables or flowers can start from seeds, so you can use these directions to plant whatever you choose. Some good flowers to grow from seeds are zinnias, snapdragons, sunflowers, marigolds, and nasturtiums. Good vegetable seeds to start are radishes, carrots, beans, lettuce, squash, watermelon, and corn. Once you have made your choice, gather your supplies and start planting!

Start seeds in paper cups, muffin tins, or egg cartons.

MATERIALS

Seeds
Egg cartons, or milk cartons cut in half lengthwise
Potting soil
Spray bottle filled with water
Plant labels

Read the directions on the seed packet. They will tell you how deep to plant your seeds. Fill the cartons with soil, poke holes in the soil with your finger or the tip of a pencil, and then drop in the seeds. Gently cover them with soil and press firmly. Spray them with a bottle of water (wash an empty bottle of spray cleaner thoroughly and fill it with water) so that the soil won't be disturbed by directly pouring the water on it.

Make plant labels (see pages 11 and 12) with the name of the plant and the date you planted the seeds. The date will let you know when to expect tiny plants to come out of the soil.

Keep the soil moist. The plants will have two leaves in the beginning. When they get their second set of leaves, they are ready to transplant into a garden or a larger pot. When you transplant, do it gently and keep the soil in place around the delicate roots. Always lift plants by the leaves, not the tiny stem.

Label them with the names of the plants and the date they were planted.

Wash out an old spray bottle and use it to keep the soil damp.

Wild Seeds

A seed is a seed: grow some "wild" plants. Gather seeds from pinecones, acorns, dandelion fluff, grasses, or weeds. Get as many different types of seed as you can. Plant them in egg cartons and wait for your wild plants.

During World War II, American people planted outdoor Victory Gardens. Those gardens provided almost half of the nation's food.

Seedling Pots

MATERIALS

Recycled typing or copier
paper, or newspaper

Tape
Scissors
Potting soil and seeds
Marker

For each pot, cut a 4-by-7-inch strip of paper. Fold it ½ inch along one long edge. Roll it into a cylinder and tape. Flatten it, and cut four 1-inch slits at the center and sides. Press it flat again to make a box shape. Fold the ends in along the slits. Tape the last flap to hold all the flaps in place.

Fill it with soil and sow the seeds. Label the pot with the name of the plant. When it's time to transplant the little plants in the garden, plant the entire pot in the ground. Gently remove the tape and open the bottom of the pot when you plant it, and the little roots will grow out easier. The paper will rot into the soil.

You can make paper pots where your seedlings will start out their lives.

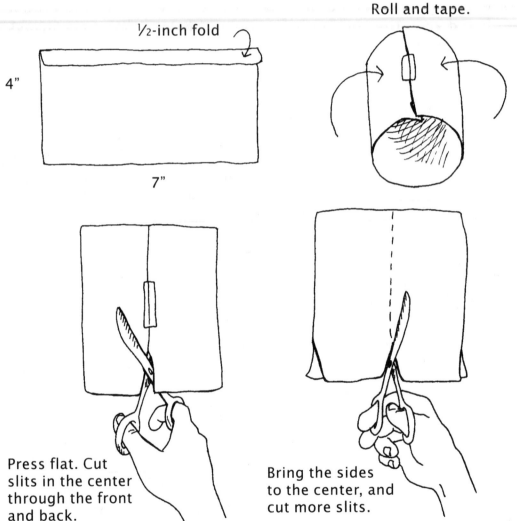

½-inch fold

4"

7"

Roll and tape.

Press flat. Cut slits in the center through the front and back.

Bring the sides to the center, and cut more slits.

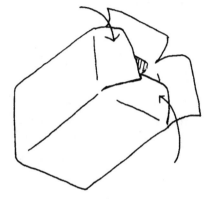

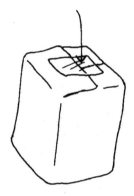

Make a box by folding the
flaps in and taping them.

Bean Bean

Fill with soil, plant seeds, and
write the plant names on the pot.

Mini Greenhouse

Y ou can make a little greenhouse to start seeds in before the last winter frosts are gone. Put it outside or on a windowsill.

Tape plastic wrap over a foil-lined shoebox.

Plant your seeds in an egg carton and put it in a clear plastic bag.

MATERIALS

Shoebox
Aluminum foil
Tape
Potting soil, seeds, and water
Plastic wrap

Line the shoebox with the foil, taping it along the rim if necessary. Fill with soil, plant the seeds, and wet the soil. Stretch the plastic wrap across the top of the box. Tape it in place. It will seal in the moisture, and if you put it in a sunny spot, it will warm the plants, too. Lift the wrap whenever you need to add water, and remove it when the plants have two sets of leaves. You can also make a greenhouse from an egg carton sealed inside a clear plastic bag.

The ancient Romans built the first greenhouses. They grew flowers in them.

Seeds in a Sack

MATERIALS

Wet paper towel
Plastic, sealable sandwich bag
Any kind of dry beans, such as
pinto, lima, or navy

Fold the towel twice, wet it, and lay it inside the bag. Place three or four bean seeds on top of the towel, and close the bag. You can leave it on a windowsill, but it's fun to thumbtack the bag to a wall and watch the bean plants emerge. When the plants have begun to get a good root system, plant them gently in soil.

Fold a wet
paper towel.

Put the towel inside a sandwich bag, add beans, and close the bag.

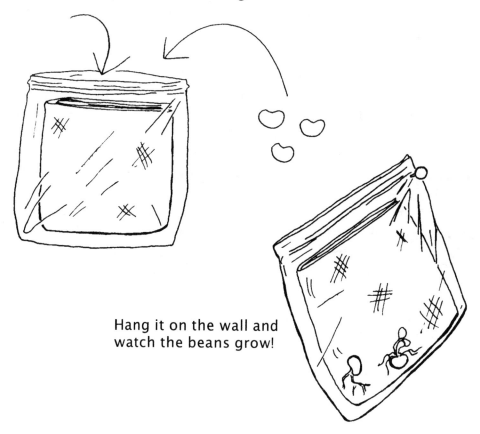

Hang it on the wall and
watch the beans grow!

It's fun and interesting to watch new plants as they burst out of their seeds and send out tiny roots.

Divide and Multiply

Even though plants grow from seeds, there are other ways you can make new plants. Many new plants will grow from stems taken from a "mother" plant. Some good ones to try are African violet, coleus, philodendron, ivy, and geranium. Plants with strong stems and leaves will usually grow from cuttings.

Use scissors to snip off a healthy stem. Take off the bottom leaves, but leave some at the end of the stem to make food. Let the cutting sit in a glass or jar of water in a sunny spot. Tiny roots will eventually develop along the cut end. The amount of time it takes depends on the plant: some will take quite a long time; others grow roots quickly. When enough roots have grown, plant the cutting in a small pot of soil, and you'll have a new plant! You can even start new rose bushes this way, using the stem from a pretty rose.

You and a few friends can each buy a different kind of plant. Share stem cuttings and everyone will have several plants for the price of one.

Root divisions can also provide new plants. When plants are several years old, they develop thick roots that can be separated. Small sections of the roots will grow into new plants. Some plants that can be grown by dividing the roots are lilies, peonies, mums, daisies, and sage. Divide the plants in late summer or fall, after the plant is finished blooming. Dig the plants up, separate the roots carefully, and then replant the roots in new flower beds.

Amazing African Violet

African violets were first found in the shady jungles of Africa. Travelers must have snipped leaves to take home with them, spreading the pretty plant around the world.

African violet plants grow easily from leaf cuttings. Clip a few outside leaves from a "mother" plant. Let them sit in a glass of water so that the stem is covered with water. Use long toothpicks or sticks to prop up the leaf and keep it from sliding down into the water. Keep it on a windowsill and in a few weeks it will have strong roots. Plant your new African violet in a small pot of soil. New leaves will grow, and eventually the plant will bloom just like the one you took the cutting from.

When it has roots, plant the leaf cutting in its own pot of soil.

Snip a leaf from an African violet plant. Let it start roots in a glass of water.

Colorful Coleus

Coleus plants are the ones with the wildly colored leaves of pink, red, yellow, purple, and chartreuse. They came from the islands of Indonesia. If you have a large coleus, you can take dozens of cuttings from it. In fact, it may eventually become a "grandparent" to lots of plants you start.

✺ Snip a stem, leave a few leaves on the end, and let it sit in a glass of water on a windowsill. In a few days, roots will begin. When the cutting has several roots, pot it in a small pot of soil and care for it with water and sunlight.

Keep your potted coleus plants indoors in the cold months, and then set some out in the yard when summer comes. They love it indoors or out. The leaf colors will change depending upon the amount of sunlight your plant receives.

Cut off a stem. Trim all but a few leaves off.

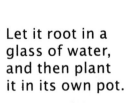

Let it root in a glass of water, and then plant it in its own pot.

Clip a leaf.

Root it in moist soil.

Jade Tree

These plants aren't really trees, but when they get older they develop beautiful brown bark that makes the Jade plant look like a tiny old tree. Older plants can grow to be as tall as a young child, and can live as long as twenty-five years.

 You can break off leaves to create cuttings. Let the leaves dry out a bit, then root them in moist soil, and create many new Jade plants. Jades don't need very much water; they store it in their thick leaves. They do need to be by a window with plenty of sunlight.

PESKY PESTS

Pests like to be in the garden, too! And every gardener has to learn to deal with them. You can use chemical sprays, but they kill friendly insects, harm birds, and eventually get into our water and make people and fish sick. Here are several ideas that will help you rid your garden of nasty pests without using harmful chemicals.

Homemade Bug Sprays

he next couple of pages have some recipes for homemade bug sprays.

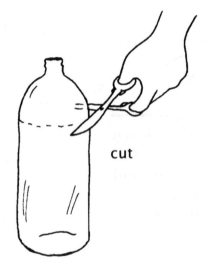

cut

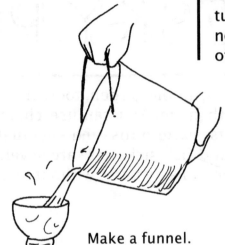

Make a funnel.

 First, you need to find something to use to spray your plants. Use the plastic spray bottles that household cleaners come in. Make sure the bottles are thoroughly washed.

An easy way to pour these mixtures into the bottle is with a funnel. You can make one by cutting off the top of a plastic bottle.

Soap Spray

You can make a spray to use on plants that are infested with insects, such as aphids or mealy bugs.

MATERIALS

½ cup soap flakes
3 gallons water
Bucket

Mix the soap flakes and water in a bucket until they are dissolved. Pour it into a clean plastic spray bottle and squirt it right on your plants.

Mix ½ cup soap flakes and 3 gallons water.

MATERIALS

Several cloves garlic
1 quart water
Garlic press or knife
Saucepan
Strainer

 Crush the garlic with a garlic press or smash it with the side of a knife. Add it to the water in a saucepan. Boil it for about five minutes, let it cool, and strain out the garlic bits. Pour the liquid into a clean spray bottle. Spray it on plants to keep insects away; it also controls fungus.

Garlic Spray

I f soapy spray doesn't get rid of the pests, here's a recipe for cooking up a stronger mixture.

Boil the garlic and water to make something that will keep the bugs away.

MATERIALS

1 teaspoon baking soda
3 drops of dishwashing liquid
2 quarts warm water
Bucket

Spray the soda spray right on your plants.

Mix the soda, soap, and water together in a bucket, and pour it into your handy spray bottle. Spray it on plants that need help fighting harmful insects.

Soda Spray

Here's another type of spray that's easy to make and uses no harmful chemicals.

Slug Trap

MATERIALS

1 teaspoon dry yeast
1 tablespoon sugar
1 cup warm water
Shallow pan with straight sides

Mix dry yeast, sugar, and water together—slugs love this concoction. Put it in a shallow pan, one that the slugs can climb up and into; a clean tuna fish can or an aluminum pan used for frozen foods are both good choices. Set out the pan early in the evening.

The slugs will come to it within minutes, fall in, and drown. Pick the dead slugs out each morning.

Slugs can't resist yeast, sugar, and water.

Slugs love to nibble the leaves of your garden plants. Since they usually come out at night, it can be very difficult to stop them. Here's a creative way to stop those pesky pests by setting a delicious trap for them.

Pest Strips

MATERIALS

Plastic milk jug
Petroleum jelly (like Vaseline)
String
Scissors
Hole punch or large nail

Use the scissors to cut long, wide strips from the milk jug. Punch a hole in one end of each strip. Tie a loop of string through the hole in the strip. Smear a thick layer of petroleum jelly on the strip. Hang it from a tree branch or a nail on the patio, and annoying flying insects will get trapped on it.

To place it next to plants in the garden, use a hot-glue gun (with grown-up help) to attach the strip to a flat stick (use a paint stirrer—they're free in the paint department). Push it in the ground next to plants that are being eaten by flying insects.

Make a simple and safe pest strip to trap flying insects that you don't want bothering you or your plants.

Cut strips from the sides of a plastic jug.

Cover the strip with petroleum jelly and hang it up.

Windmills

Some gardens are bothered by birds, such as crows, that love to eat the seeds right out of the ground—after you just planted them! To scare them away until the plants get big, you might try windmills. These little windmills will also keep raccoons and deer from coming into the garden and eating their fill!

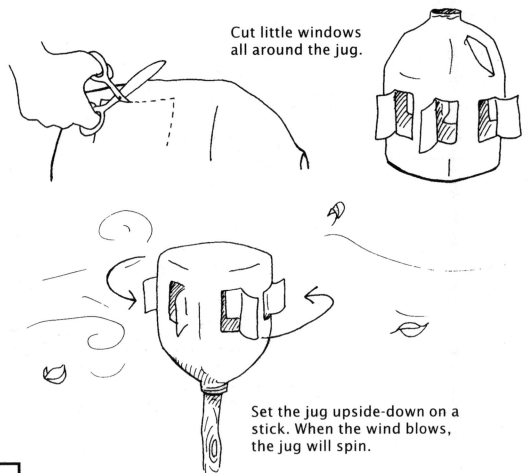

Cut little windows all around the jug.

Set the jug upside-down on a stick. When the wind blows, the jug will spin.

MATERIALS

Plastic milk jug
3-foot stake or stick
Scissors

❀ Use the scissors to cut out little windows in the sides of the jug as shown in the drawing. Bend the cutouts outward and crease them so that they stay open. Perch the cutout bottle on a stake, upside down, near the plants you want to protect.

The wind will catch in the little cutouts and spin the jug round and round, rattling and spooking animals who don't know what it is.

Problems with ants? Sprinkle catnip on their path and they'll turn around and leave! Use mint to keep mice away. Grow it in your herb garden or a windowsill pot. Place long stems of it in the attic.

MATERIALS

Plastic milk jug
Acrylic paints and paintbrush
Old broomstick
3-foot dowel or stick
Heavy twine or wire

Old clothing: pants and shirt
(and shoes, if you like)

Newspaper
Rubber bands

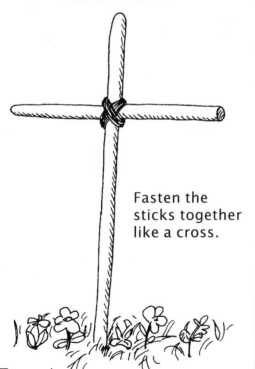

Fasten the sticks together like a cross.

Windmills might not be enough to scare some brave animal pests. Make a scarecrow to keep them out of your growing garden. Birds and animals will think it is a person standing watch over the crops. Clothes will make the scarecrow seem more real to them because the birds will smell the human odor left on them. Gather together some old clothing and get started.

Paint a face on the jug.

Add a drop of dishwashing liquid to the paint so that it sticks to the plastic.

Paint the outside of the jug with flesh-colored acrylic paint. If the paint won't stick to the plastic, adding a drop of dishwashing liquid to the paint will help. Paint large eyes, a nose, and a mouth using bright red and black.

Go out to your garden and push the handle of the broomstick into the ground. Use twine or flexible wire to fasten the stick and dowel together into a cross. Dress it with old clothing, stuffing the clothes full of crumpled newspapers to give it body. Use rubber bands to keep the stuffing in place. Lower the jug head onto the broomstick end.

Add a hat, work gloves, old boots, or anything else you can think of that will make your scarecrow seem like a real person.

Dress the scarecrow in old clothing stuffed with newspapers.

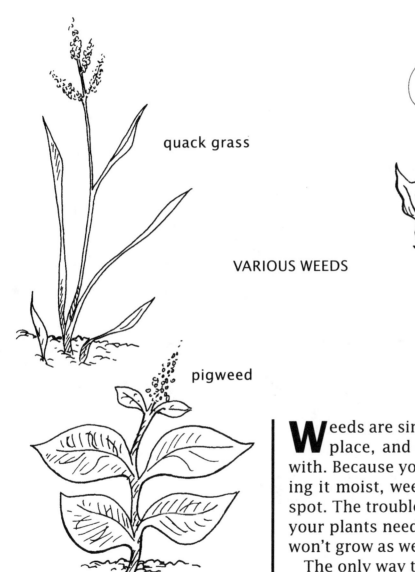

quack grass

VARIOUS WEEDS

dandelion

pigweed

Weeds are simply plants that happen to be growing in the wrong place, and they are another garden pest you'll have to deal with. Because you've done such a good job tilling the soil and keeping it moist, weed seeds will plant themselves in your nice garden spot. The trouble with weeds is that they will soak up moisture that your plants need and will crowd their roots and leaves. Your plants won't grow as well if they are surrounded by wild weed plants.

The only way to get rid of them once they have sprouted is to pull them up—root and all.

By far, the best way to deal with weeds is to prevent them from growing in the first place. To keep them out, you can put down a layer or a blanket of material that will keep the weed seeds from settling in the soil and starting to grow. This layer of material is called "mulch." Mulches can be made from many things: sawdust, straw, chipped bark, grass clippings, or old, shredded newspaper.

Whatever you use, you can prevent weeds before they begin to grow by laying a blanket of mulch around your plants. The weeds won't get any sunlight and mulch keeps the soil from drying out quickly.

Lay a blanket of mulch around your plants to keep the weeds from growing.

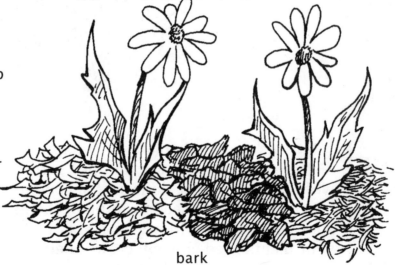

newspaper

bark

grass clippings

GARDEN PARTNERS

Not *all* bugs, birds, and animals will harm your garden. There are many that will be your helpers. There are "good" insects that will eat the "bad" insects that will harm your plants.

Birds eat hundreds of insects each day and will help you keep the insect population under control in your yard and garden.

Bats eat insects that come out at night when birds are at rest. They make their homes in dark places high off the ground. Watch outdoors in the early summer evening and you may see them swooping and flying about near treetops, rooftops, and utility poles. They're out snacking on flying insects.

Bats love to feed on flying insects.

Other animals will help you out, too. Toads and frogs eat slugs that can chew up plants overnight. Lizards dine on small insects and their larvae. Snakes and spiders help out. Snakes eat slugs, and spiders catch insects in their webs. Earthworms contribute by working through the soil, enriching and loosening it so plants grow better. Butterflies and bees lend a hand by going from blossom to blossom, carrying pollen along as they travel.

Frogs and toads are garden helpers.

Insects stick
to a spider's
web and
become the
spider's dinner.

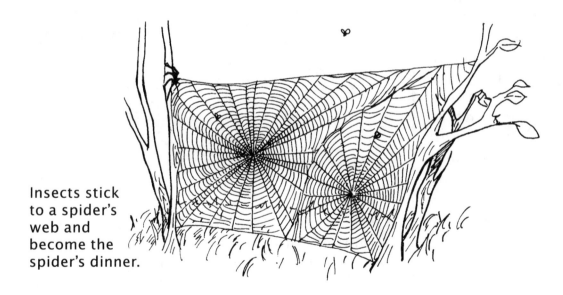

So, when you plan your garden project, you should also plan ways to get your animal helpers into the garden with you. Here are some things you can do.

Build a Birdhouse

MATERIALS

Large plastic milk jug
Dowel or stick
Heavy twine
Rocks
Bird seed
Bits of grass
Pointed scissors
Large nail

 Cut out a small round opening in the side of the jug for the bird to enter. Use the nail to work a small hole below the larger opening and push the stick in to make a perch. Work two more holes near the top of the jug and thread the twine through. Knot and tie a long loop. Hang the birdhouse up on a sturdy tree branch. Put a few rocks inside to weight the house so it won't blow in the wind.

You can also make birdhouses by hollowing out dried gourds and hanging them from tree branches.

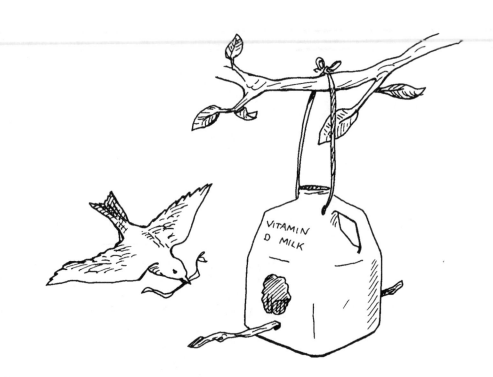

You needed a scarecrow to keep seed-eating birds out of the garden, but you'll want to encourage insect-eating birds to come into the garden. Some birds that will eat insects are the titmouse, chickadee, nuthatch, robin, warbler, bluebird, wren, starling, waxwing, oriole, and gnatcatcher.

Wherever birds nest, they will busily hunt insects to feed to their baby hatchlings. You can attract them by making a comfortable place for them to make a home.

Try cutting one out of a milk carton. Use a hot-glue gun (with grown-up help) to attach a metal pie tin to the bottom so that the birds have a ledge to stand on when they enter and leave the house.

Sprinkle some birdseed and a bit of dry grass inside the house, and wait for the new neighbors to move in!

Cut holes in clean milk cartons or jugs. Add sticks for perches.

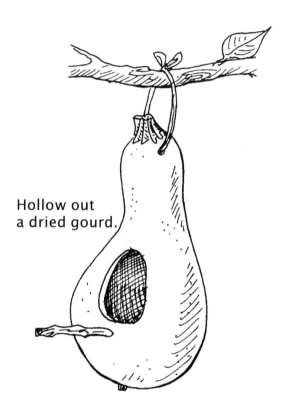

Hollow out a dried gourd.

MATERIALS

Plastic 1-liter bottle
(from soda pop)

Aluminum pie plate
(from frozen foods)

Thin wire or twine

Large nail or pointed scissors

Heavy-duty glue
(or hot-glue gun
with grown-up help)

To keep helpful birds around, you'll want to provide them some tasty snacks. Some insect-eating birds like to eat seeds; others prefer suet mixtures. Suet, or pinecones rolled in peanut butter and birdseed, will attract insect-eating birds to your yard.

Here's one way to make a birdfeeder that can be filled with different sorts of seed.

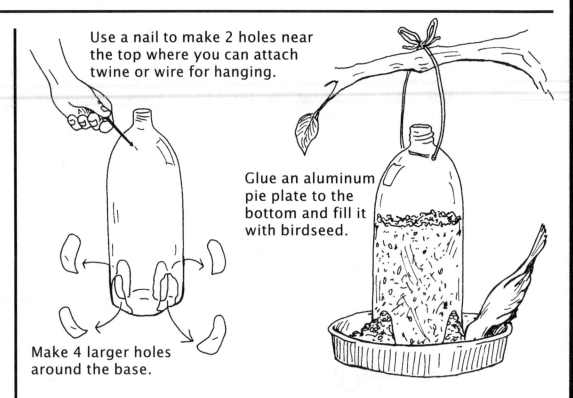

Use a nail to make 2 holes near the top where you can attach twine or wire for hanging.

Make 4 larger holes around the base.

Glue an aluminum pie plate to the bottom and fill it with birdseed.

Wash the bottle and let the inside of it dry completely. Use the nail or the point of the scissors to punch two holes in the top of the bottle. Push the piece of wire or twine through and form a hanging loop. Use the nail to make large holes around the bottom in four places. Use the scissors to work the holes large enough so that the seed will easily fall out. Glue the bottle to the aluminum pie plate. Use the nail to poke three or four holes in the bottom of the pie plate to let rain drain out. Fill the feeder with birdseed and set it out on a tree branch or hang from a hook on the patio roof.

Remember: When you start feeding birds, they will begin to rely on that food. If you stop, they may starve. Once you begin a feeding program, you must keep it up, especially during the winter months when the birds have few other things to eat.

 Plant some food for the birds, too. Start some sunflowers in a sunny spot next to a wall, fence, or building. They will grow taller than you and will have huge blossoms full of seeds that the birds will find delicious. When the flower heads ripen, birds will snack the seeds right off the plant. When fall comes, cut off the sunflower heads and let them dry indoors. Use the seeds to fill birdfeeders all winter. Toast a few for yourself in a low-temperature oven (200 degrees) for about 15 minutes.

Tantalize all types of birds into visiting your garden by growing plants that have berries and fruits that birds like to eat. Bayberry bushes, bittersweet, Virginia Creeper vines, cherry trees, and crabapple trees all provide "berried treasure" for birds.

Another way to attract birds is to set out some nesting materials for them in the spring. Save pieces of yarn, thread, shredded cloth, cotton balls, and even clothes dryer lint. Drape the supplies on low-hanging tree or shrub branches where birds will see it. Later, when the nests are empty in summer, take an exploring trip around the neighborhood, looking for nests made with some of your supplies.

You can attract birds with a birdbath, too. Place a large pan full of cool water in a shady spot where cats and dogs won't bother them.

Make a Garden Pond

 rogs, toads, lizards, salamanders, and snakes eat insects and slugs that can damage your garden. A little pond will keep frogs in the area. You can also add some special water plants, and even a few goldfish! Goldfish love to eat mosquito larvae, but be sure to feed them fish food, too.

Use a wading pool to make a garden pond.

A simple pond can be made by digging a hole to fit a small wading pool or plastic tub. You can use a baby bathtub, a large dishpan, or even a new cat litter box to make a small pond. Dig a hole to sink it into the ground. A shady spot is best for the animals and plants that will drink from it. Also, the water won't get too hot and won't dry up as fast if it's in the shade. Lay pretty rocks around the edge, and plant a few ferns or some moss near the edge. Keep the area wet, and be sure the little pond is always filled with water. Frogs may come to visit, and birds may bathe in it. When winter comes, bring the goldfish indoors in a fish bowl until spring.

Butterfly Garden

Butterflies help out in the garden by pollinating plants as they travel from flower to flower. In a sunny spot in the garden, you can create a special place where they can enjoy themselves. Plant flowers that produce lots of sweet nectar for them to eat. Flowers with purple, yellow, or orange blossoms attract them. Flowers with short petals or flat tops make it easy for them to land and feed easily. Place large flat stones in the garden because butterflies like to sit and bask in the sun. Make sure there is a little puddle or birdbath for them to drink from.

Butterflies lay eggs that hatch into caterpillars. When the caterpillars are fully grown, they make a chrysalis, go to sleep inside it, and emerge again as butterflies. Butterfly mothers are very choosy about where they lay their eggs. They want to be sure the little caterpillars will be able to eat the plant the eggs hatch on. Plant parsley, carrots, dill, and beans for the larvae (caterpillars) to eat.

Butterflies enjoy zinnias.

Butterflies lay eggs on plants that the larvae can eat when they hatch.

Here are some plants that butterflies will come to: hollyhocks, marigolds, nasturtiums, violets, asters, and zinnias. They can all be grown from seeds. There are larger shrubs called "Butterfly Bush" (Buddleia) and lilacs that you may want to plant in your butterfly garden, too.

Want to raise butterflies? You can buy larvae and kits from these scientific supply companies:

Carolina Biological Supply
2700 York Road
Burlington, NC 27215
(1-800-334-5551)

Connecticut Valley
Biological Supply
P.O. Box 326
Southampton, MA 01073

Monarch butterflies will only lay eggs on milkweed plants. Think twice before pulling them up as "weeds." You can tell it's milkweed if white sap oozes out of the broken stem.

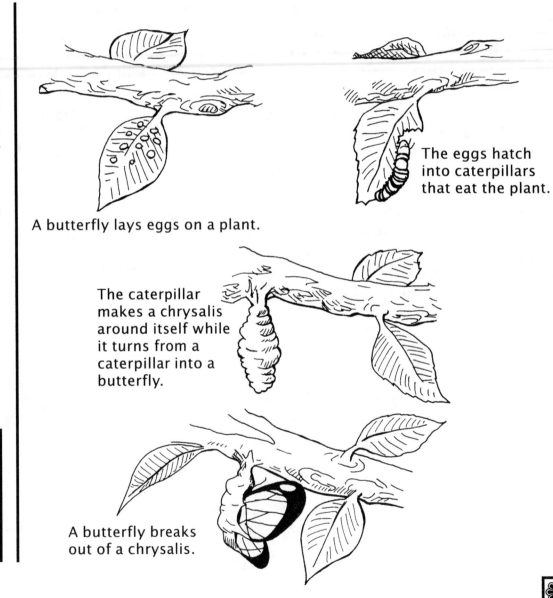

A butterfly lays eggs on a plant.

The eggs hatch into caterpillars that eat the plant.

The caterpillar makes a chrysalis around itself while it turns from a caterpillar into a butterfly.

A butterfly breaks out of a chrysalis.

Bring on the Bees

Bees do lots of work in the garden. They are busy getting flower nectar to make honey with back at their homes. As they travel from flower to flower, their tiny bodies get covered with pollen. (Look inside a flower for that yellow dust—that's pollen.) As they travel, the bees mix pollen between plants, leaving a bit here and picking up a bit there. This mixing of pollen causes trees and plants to "set" fruit, such as apples and zucchini. Without pollinating, many plant blossoms will never form into seeds.

To attract honeybees, you can plant these: borage, chamomile, chives, lavender, oregano, sage, and thyme. All can be started from seeds in the garden. Blue seems to be the bee's favorite flower color.

Some people don't like bees because they sting. Bees sting when they are protecting their nests or when they feel in danger. When you are in the flower garden, check a blossom before you grab it. A bee may be working inside the petals.

Have you ever opened a bean pod or pea pod and found it empty? That's what happens when a pea blossom isn't fertilized with pollen by a bee or butterfly.

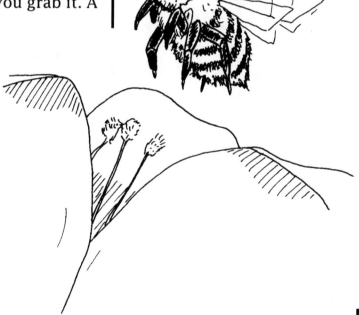

Other Insect Friends

There are many insects that help the gardener by eating other insects that damage plants. That's one good reason not to spray your garden with harmful chemical pesticides. Pesticides kill *all* insects, both good and bad.

The praying mantis eats only live insects.

Praying Mantis

The praying mantis is a wonderful-looking character with long legs and bulging eyes; they will eat lots of cutworms, beetles, flies, aphids, and insect eggs. Each mantis will eat many times its own weight each day. It got its name because it holds its front legs as if it's praying. However, because the mantis eats so many other insects (and only eats them when they are alive), it should be called "preying"!

Look carefully in your garden to see if you already have a mantis or two. If not, you can purchase the egg cases from garden supply catalogs or through garden stores. Gurney's (see Addresses, page 127.) will mail egg cases. Each egg case holds about 300 eggs. Don't expect to have 300 praying mantises in your garden because not all of them will hatch, and many will be eaten by birds or leave your yard. When they hatch from the egg case, they will be the size of mosquitoes, and it will take about five months for them to grow to their full size.

If you want to watch the tiny insects hatch from the egg case, you can do that indoors. Keep the egg case in the refrigerator. Two weeks before warm weather (the end of April or first part of May), bring the egg case out in a clean glass jar with a tight-fitting lid. Prepare the jar lid ahead of time by punching several air holes in it with a nail. Stretch a piece cut from some nylon stockings over the top of the jar, and place the lid on top of that. That will keep the tiny insects from escaping through the holes and running around your house.

After they hatch, which takes about 3 weeks at room temperature, you can watch them for a day or so, but you must release them in the garden so they can find food. The mantises that survive and remain in your yard will lay egg cases in the fall, and new ones will hatch in the spring.

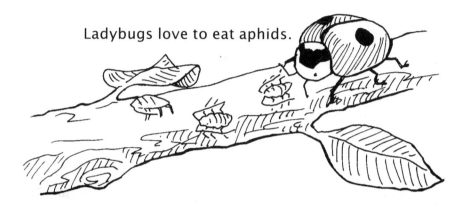

Ladybugs love to eat aphids.

Ladybugs

Ladybugs are great garden helpers, too. They feast on mites, aphids, and mealy bugs—insects that suck juices out of your plants. Each ladybug eats up to two dozen insects a day! If you find any in your garden, treat them carefully. If you need some for your plants, order them from a garden catalog or garden center. The ladybugs will come in the mail in a small, pint-sized box when the weather is warm in your area.

Ladybugs are migratory insects. They travel to certain areas for the winter where they hibernate until spring.

Have you heard the old rhyme, "Ladybug, ladybug, fly away home. Your house is on fire, your children do roam"? In the Middle Ages in England, hop fields were burned at the end of each growing season. The fire cleared the fields, but it also killed the ladybugs. This is why children said this rhyme. People also thought ladybugs were good medicine for curing measles and toothaches.

Green Lacewings

Here's another hungry pest eater. Green lacewings eat red spiders, aphids, mealy bugs, thrips, scale, and more. You can order them, too, and release them in your garden where they will lay eggs for the next season. They're a gardener's pal.

To keep insect helpers happy, you might want to include some of the plants they most enjoy in your garden. Cosmos, marigolds, zinnias, nasturtium, dill, spearmint, and clover will keep the "good" insects coming back to your yard.

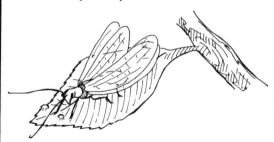

Green lacewings eat red spiders, aphids, mealy bugs, thrips, and scale.

Wonderful Worms

Earthworms are a gardener's best friend. They "eat" garden soil and rotting plant material, and pass the castings out. This loosens hard soil and adds valuable plant food, too. Give worms a home in a compost heap. They will make their home near the bottom, where they can digest the rotting plant materials.

If your garden soil doesn't contain many worms, you can purchase them from a fishing supply shop. Loosen soil before you gently lower them into the garden. Mulch the worm bed with a layer of rotting leaves, grass clippings, vegetable waste, and torn newspapers. Keep it moist so the materials don't dry out.

The worms will work away, turning the waste materials into super garden soil. Their work will also open up the ground, letting air enter and plant roots spread out.

Earthworms lay eggs and grow during the spring. When the soil dries out and heats up in summer most of the adults die off. To keep your earthworms active in the summer, keep a spot wet for them, with a layer of mulch to let them hide from the heat.

Today's most common type of earthworm in the United States originally came with the early settlers from Europe, probably in the soil that the plants they brought came in.

You can tell how old an earthworm is by counting the segments in its body. An adult worm has about 100.

Long ago, people thought a man and woman would fall in love if they ate periwinkle leaves ground up with earthworms!

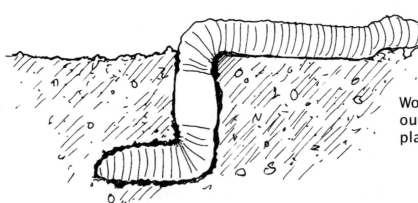

Worms eat the soil and pass out the castings, which helps plants grow better.

Helpful Plants

Carrots grow better when planted near lettuce and chives.

chives

Carrots

lettuce

It's hard to believe that *plants* can protect each other from insects, but it's true! If particular plants grow next to one other, they can keep harmful insects away. Some plants have special odors, oils, or colors that insects don't like to be near. Certain plants will make others grow better and give bigger vegetables or flowers. Learn which plants are pals for each other, and plant them together in your garden.

Roses like garlic and parsley.

Tomatoes like basil and parsley.

Cabbage likes dill and sage, but don't put it near tomatoes.

Carrots like lettuce and chives. (Don't put dill near carrots—they won't grow very large.)

Radishes like nasturtiums.

Asparagus likes tomatoes.

TASTY IDEAS

I t's fun to grow plants for birds, butterflies, and bees, but it's even more fun to grow plants that *you* can eat. Growing your own food helps you understand more about what you eat. When you garden, you know where your food comes from and how it is grown; this makes eating it more satisfying. As any gardener knows, nothing tastes as good as something you've grown yourself.

Sprout Farm

The best thing about working with plants is that you end up with some tasty food when it's time to harvest. But that takes time. While you're waiting for the vegetables to ripen in the garden, you can sprout some seeds for eating within a few days.

Use a rubber band to cover the jar of beans with nylon netting.

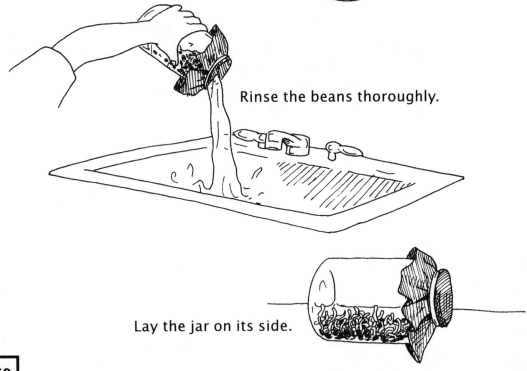

Rinse the beans thoroughly.

Lay the jar on its side.

MATERIALS

Seeds to sprout:
mung beans, alfalfa, or lentils

Quart or pint glass jar

Nylon netting or piece cut from nylon stockings

Rubber band

Water

❀ Measure out a few tablespoons of seeds, and put them in the jar. Secure the netting over the top with the rubber band. Fill the jar with water and then pour it out. Do this three or four times so that the seeds are completely rinsed. Let the jar rest on its side.

Rinse and drain the seeds three times a day. In just a few days, the seeds will sprout. Continue rinsing and draining until the sprouts are the size you like.

Add them to cottage cheese, salads, and sandwiches. Crunchy goodness, and full of vitamins. If you want to store them, put them in a covered plastic container in the refrigerator.

Chinese Stir Fry

Here's a recipe that uses vegetables from your garden, and bean sprouts, too.

Some plants can make you very sick: poison ivy and poison oak are harmful to touch. Plants like poinsettias, mistletoe, and oleander are poisonous. Never eat any part of a plant without checking it with an adult first.

INGREDIENTS

Fresh vegetables:
celery, carrots, onion, broccoli, green peppers, cauliflower, and green beans

Bean sprouts
2 tablespoons cooking oil

UTENSILS

Knife
Frying pan or wok
Cooking spoon

 You can use all of the vegetables listed, or only a few. Wash and cut them into small pieces. Heat the oil in a frying pan or wok, with a grown-up's help. Stir and fry the vegetables for a few minutes. Toss in the sprouts and cook for a few minutes more.

That's it! You can also eat stir-fried vegetables with rice or noodles.

Eat Your Flowers!

People have eaten flowers for a long time. Chinese cooks have used lotus blossoms and chrysanthemums in their recipes for centuries.

CAUTION: Be sure you know which flowers are safe to eat. Some plants are poisonous, so be sure to ask an adult who knows. *Do not eat:* **foxglove, daffodil, iris, lily, milkweed, mistletoe, narcissus, tomato plants, eggplant plants, potato leaves or blossoms, oleander, poinsettia, poppy—and many others. Be sure to ask someone to identify the plants for you.**

CAUTION: Be sure the garden spot has not been sprayed with chemicals or pesticides. They can make you very sick.

Here are some good flower choices for eating: dandelions, nasturtium, rose petals, zucchini blossoms, pansies, and violets.

Pick them in the morning when the blossoms are fresh and moist. Pull off the stem and leaves. Rinse the blossoms in cold water and drain them in a colander. Wrap in damp paper towels and put in a self-locking plastic bag. Store them in the refrigerator until you are ready to eat them.

You can toss edible flowers in salads, decorate frosted cakes, or even freeze the petals in ice cubes to freshen your punch.

Nasturtium Salad

ere's a recipe for a colorful salad made with flowers.

People used to make cheese its yellow color by mixing in marigold blossoms.

INGREDIENTS

1 package lemon-flavored gelatin
2 handfuls nasturtium blossoms
2 cups miniature marshmallows
Sprig fresh mint or parsley

 Pick off the stems and rinse the blossoms. Prepare the gelatin following the directions on the package, and let it thicken a bit in the refrigerator. Stir in the marshmallows and flower blossoms. Chill until firm. Decorate each serving with a fresh blossom and a sprig of fresh mint or parsley.

Mix together the gelatin, flowers, and marshmallows.

Decorate each serving with a nasturtium blossom and fresh parsley.

Flower Petal Candy

INGREDIENTS

Fresh violet or rose petals,*
or use mint leaves

2 tablespoons meringue powder
4 teaspoons water
Sugar

* Be sure they are not covered
with pesticides—do not use
flowers from the florist

UTENSILS

Mixing bowl
Mixing spoon
Paper towels
Waxed paper

There are about 20,000 edible plants in the world, but not all are eaten.

The fruit of a plant develops where the flower grew. The petals fall off as the flower grows into a fruit or seed pod. Look at an apple. Can you find where the blossom used to be?

Here's how you can turn fresh flower petals into a sweet treat. Use them to pretty-up a frosted cake or cupcakes. People decorated their desserts with these candied petals 200 years ago.

Mix together the meringue powder and water. Wash fresh rose or violet petals, or mint leaves, and dry them on a paper towel. Dip them one at a time in the meringue mixture. Spread them on waxed paper and sprinkle sugar on top. Let them dry an hour or so until they harden.

Dip the flower petals in the mixture.

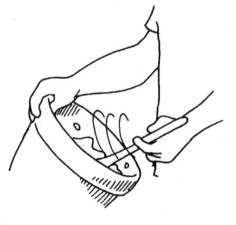

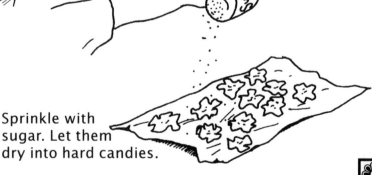

Sprinkle with sugar. Let them dry into hard candies.

Carrot Cake

Carrot cake is delicious with vanilla icing!

INGREDIENTS

2 eggs
1 ½ cups flour
1 cup raw shredded carrot
1 cup sugar
⅔ cup cooking oil
1 teaspoon baking powder
1 teaspoon baking soda
1 teaspoon cinnamon
1 tablespoon vanilla

UTENSILS

Mixing bowl
Mixing spoon
Greased, 8-inch, square baking pan
Toothpick

Carrots grow quickly, and, if you planted lots of seeds, you may have a bountiful harvest. Use them in this recipe for delicious carrot cake.

 Stir the flour, sugar, baking powder, baking soda, and cinnamon together in a large bowl. Add the eggs, carrot, oil, and vanilla. Stir for about three minutes until it's mixed thoroughly.

Prepare the baking pan by greasing it with shortening and then sprinkling 1 tablespoon of flour over it. Shake the pan until it is coated. This will keep the cake from sticking to the pan.

Preheat the oven to 350 degrees. Bake the cake for about 35 minutes. Test to see if it's done in the center by poking a toothpick into it. If the toothpick comes out clean, the cake is done.

Vegetable Soup

INGREDIENTS

2 or 3 cups of
chopped raw vegetables:
carrot, potato, onion, squash,
turnip, broccoli, celery,
and tomato

2 cans beef or chicken bouillon

Salt and pepper

Herbs:
oregano, garlic, chives,
rosemary, or whatever you like

UTENSILS

Knife
Large saucepan
Cooking spoon

Mmmm!

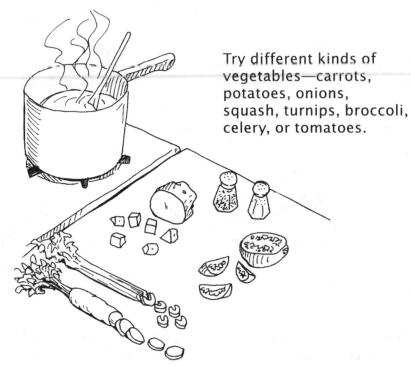

Try different kinds of vegetables—carrots, potatoes, onions, squash, turnips, broccoli, celery, or tomatoes.

You can use all your garden vegetables to make some scrumptious soup. You can choose which vegetables you want to use, but it's best to use at least three kinds.

Cut the vegetables into small bite-sized pieces. Heat the bouillon in a saucepan, and add the vegetables, salt, and pepper. While it's heating up, sprinkle chopped herbs—a tablespoon or so—into the broth to add flavor. Let the soup simmer for about half an hour.

The best thing about vegetable soup is that you can create something different every time, depending on what vegetables you choose!

FUN WITH HERBS

Herbs are special plants that have many uses. Herbs, such as chives, dill, and basil are added to food to give it delicious flavors. Other herbs, such as mint and chamomile, are used to make teas. They are also used for their fragrance, to keep insect pests away, and other useful things. Herbs have been used as medicine for centuries. You can grow herbs in pots sitting on a windowsill or hanging on a patio, or in a garden spot.

Some herbs that grow easily are chives, dill, basil, parsley, mint, and sage. Plant the seeds in small pots or egg cartons, and then leave the pots in a warm sunny spot. Keep the soil moist. When the plants grow larger they can be planted outdoors or in larger pots.

When you want to season your dinner, just pick a few leaves off of your herb plant. Snip the leaves with scissors or crush them with your fingers to release the flavoring oils.

Most herbs grow back year after year in the garden, so you don't have to replant them every year. Herbs can also be multiplied by root division; so, when you have a large plant, you can dig it up and separate the roots into smaller clumps to start new plants. Be sure the root piece is at least 2 inches long, and replant it carefully (see Divide & Multiply, page 26).

Start your herb garden in an egg carton.

Immigrants brought herbs to America with them. The English brought mint and thyme. Germans brought dill. Italians brought bay plants. Mint came from the Middle East.

In biblical times, people paid their taxes with dill and mint, instead of money.

VARIOUS HERBS

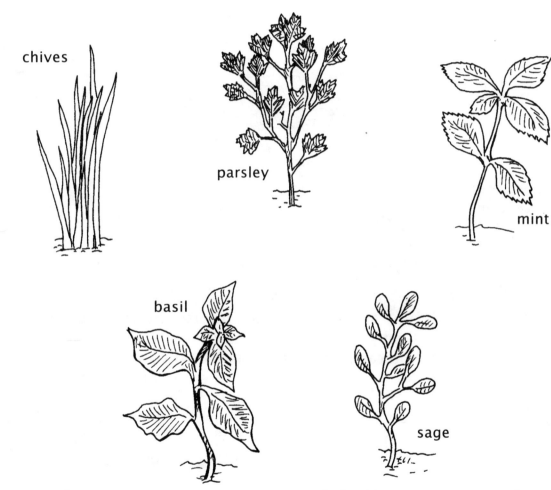

chives

parsley

mint

basil

sage

Herbs are tasty in soup, stew, or salads. Try oregano on a cheese pizza, or chopped dill on tuna sandwiches. Yummy! There are many ways to use your harvest of herbs.

MATERIALS

Screen Herb Dryer

Old wooden picture frame

Old window screen

Tacks and hammer (or staple gun with grown-up help)

Hanging Herb Dryer

Clothes hanger

Rubber bands

Did you know that spices come from plants, too? Cinnamon is bark from a tree. Cloves are flower buds. Allspice is a berry. Nutmeg is a fruit pit. Vanilla is a flower seed pod. All of them grow only in warm, tropical climates.

Hang the herbs from a hanger with rubber bands.

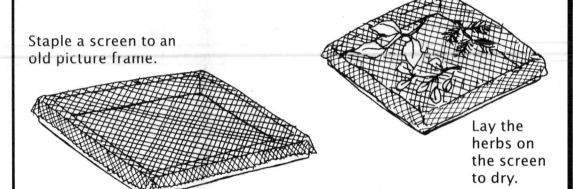

Staple a screen to an old picture frame.

Lay the herbs on the screen to dry.

There are two ways to prepare herbs for drying. You can spread the leaves on a drying screen that you make yourself or hang them. Here are instructions for both ways.

To make your own screen dryer, stretch the piece of screen across the frame and use the tacks and hammer to fasten it tightly to the sides. Put tacks every inch or so around the entire frame. You can also use a staple gun, if you have grown-up help. Place your fresh herbs on top and let them air-dry in a cool, dark place.

You can also hang your herbs to dry. Gather the herb stems in small bundles and use rubber bands to hang them on clothes hangers. Let them hang in a dry, dark place for a few weeks.

When your herbs are dry to the touch, gently take the leaves off the stems and store the leaves in glass jars, plastic bags, or plastic containers with tight lids. You'll always have herbs to use when you're cooking. The following pages have great recipes that use herbs.

Dried herbs also make great gifts, too. Decorate the containers you put them in to make them special (see Pretty Herb Jars, page 78.)

MATERIALS

4 tea bags
1-gallon glass or clear plastic jug
Water
1 cup honey or sugar
2 handfuls spearmint, lemon verbena, or peppermint leaves

 Fill the jug with water. Add one cup of honey or sugar and two handfuls of spearmint, lemon verbena, or peppermint leaves, or a combination of these. Put in four regular tea bags. Fill the jug in the morning and let it sit in the sun all day. By dinnertime, the tea will be ready. Stir it, strain it into glasses, and add ice cubes.

Make some tea without boiling water—use solar power!

Herb Tea

Put a handful of chamomile blossoms, mint leaves, or lemon balm in a teapot. Pour two cups of boiling water over it. Let it sit for 5 to 10 minutes. Add a spoonful of honey or sugar to sweeten it. You can use only one herb, or mix them for a special blend.

In the Middle Ages many people grew "medicinal gardens," which were filled with herbs that were used as medicine.

Honey

INGREDIENTS

5 or 6 fresh tomatoes
1 cup vinegar
1 cup salad oil
Fresh herbs

UTENSILS

Shallow pan
Jar with lid

Combine fresh tomatoes and herbs from your garden with oil and vinegar, and you'll have a healthy taste treat.

Slice fresh tomatoes from your garden into a shallow pan. Sprinkle them with chopped chives, basil, and any other herbs you like. In a jar with a lid, mix one cup vinegar and one cup salad oil. Shake it until the two are mixed. Pour the dressing over the tomatoes, add more herbs if you like, and refrigerate until the tomatoes are cold.

People once thought tomatoes were poisonous, and that eating eggplant would make you insane!

Herbed Eggs

INGREDIENTS

Hard-boiled eggs
Mayonnaise
(I tablespoon for each egg)
Fresh chives and dill, chopped
Parsley

UTENSILS

Knife
Small bowl
Fork
Spoon

Remove the shells from the eggs. Slice them in half lengthwise. Mix the yolks, mayonnaise, and herbs in a small bowl with a fork. Spoon the mixture back into the egg whites. Stick a few sprigs of fresh parsley from your garden on the plate to make it pretty.

Cut the eggs in half lengthwise, and take out the yolks.

Mix the yolks with mayonnaise and herbs.

Fill the egg white with the yolk mixture, and decorate them with parsley.

Herbed Butter

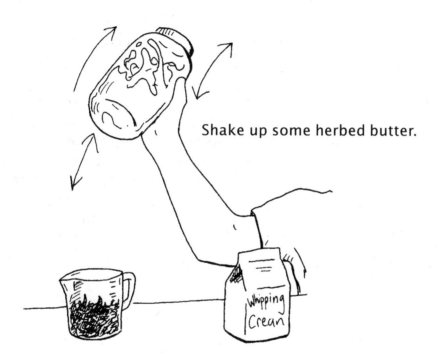

Shake up some herbed butter.

INGREDIENTS

1 pint whipping cream
½ cup chopped fresh basil,
   parsley, chives,
   marjoram, or oregano

UTENSILS

Jar with lid
Fork

 Put the whipping cream in the jar and close the lid securely. Shake the jar back and forth until the cream turns solid and becomes butter. Pour off the watery "buttermilk." Use a fork to mash the butter and blend in the herbs. Roll the butter into a ball with your hands. Set it on a plate with fresh parsley. This is great on baked potatoes.

Dill Dip

INGREDIENTS

1 cup mayonnaise

1 cup sour cream

1 tablespoon onion, chopped

2 tablespoons dill weed, chopped

1 teaspoon salt

Mix everything together in a small bowl. Wash and slice raw vegetables from your garden, such as carrots, celery, zucchini, and cauliflower. Dip the raw veggies in the dip for a tasty, healthy snack.

Chop some onion and dill, and add sour cream and mayonnaise for a great dip.

INGREDIENTS

8-ounce package cream cheese, softened

½ stick margarine

2 teaspoons lemon juice

2 teaspoons fresh sage, chopped (or 1 teaspoon dried)

 Mix everything together in a bowl. This special herbed treat is delicious spread on crackers or toast.

Mix cream cheese, margarine, lemon juice, and fresh sage for a spread that is good on toast or crackers.

MATERIALS

Jar with lid
Fabric scraps
Ribbon or yarn
Pencil
Scissors
Rubber band

 Look for little glass jars with lids. Baby food jars are perfect, but you might discover others, too. Little plastic bottles with snap-on lids that pills come in make nice containers.

Pack dry herbs into the jars and cap tightly. Make some pretty labels for the containers, and tape or glue them in place.

Draw a circle on the fabric about an inch larger than the jar's lid. Cut it out and wrap it over the jar with the lid attached. Secure it with a rubber band. Tie ribbon or yarn over the rubber band to hide it. Tie on a tiny card to go with your herb gift.

Homegrown herbs make great gifts. A pretty jar topper and package will make your herb gift unique.

Hide the rubber band with some ribbon.

A pretty gift you make yourself.

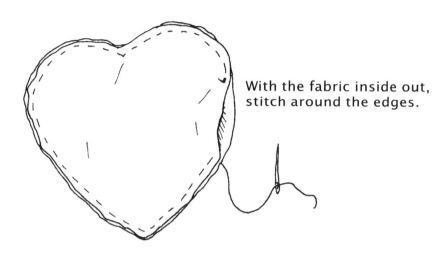

With the fabric inside out, stitch around the edges.

Woven fabric:
calico, gingham, or broadcloth
(or use a pretty handkerchief folded in half)

Dried herbs

Needle and thread (or a sewing machine with grown-up help)

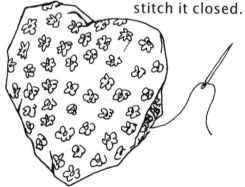

Stuff the pillow with herbs, and stitch it closed.

Make a tiny pillow filled with fragrant herbs. Don't make yours too large; make it just small enough to hold near your nose for a sniff now and then.

✿ Cut the fabric into two identical squares, rectangles, or heart shapes. With the wrong sides facing out, stitch around the outer edges, leaving about an inch unstitched. Turn the pillow right-side out and fill it with dry herbs. You can add uncooked dry rice to the herb mixture if you don't have enough herbs to fill the pillow. Stitch the opening closed with a needle and thread.

Mix lavender, marjoram, dried rose petals, and ground cloves together to make a "headache" pillow. Sniffing it should help headaches go away.

Make a "sleep" pillow to help you get to sleep on those nights when counting sheep just won't do it! Fill the little pillow with dried rose petals, mint leaves, and crushed cloves.

At castle banquets long ago, guests were given bowls of water scented with fresh rosemary leaves to wash their hands in.

MATERIALS

⅓ cup water
1 ⅓ cups soap flakes
(Ivory or White King brand)
2 tablespoons dried lavender
or lemon verbena

Fabric scraps
Ribbon
Saucepan
Cooking spoon

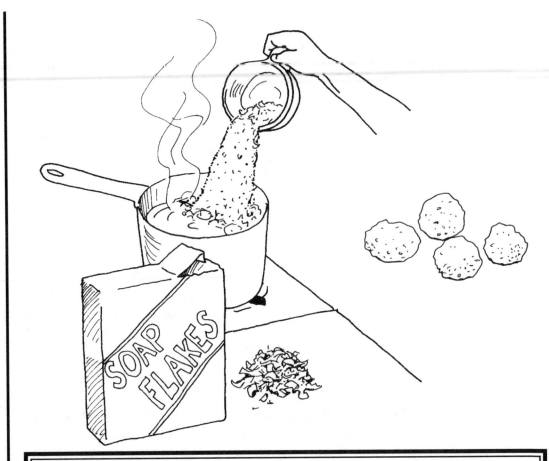

Heat the water in a saucepan. Add the dried lavender or lemon verbena and simmer for five minutes. Add the soap and stir. Stir until the soap flakes dissolve into a creamy mixture. Remove it from the heat. When the mixture is cool enough, shape it into soap balls the size of golf balls. Let the soap balls set for a week to age and harden. Wrap them in scraps of pretty fabric tied with a ribbon.

The kings and queens of England had a Royal Herb Strewer. Their job was to toss sweet-smelling plants on the floors of the castle. It made the rooms smell fresh, and kept bugs and mice out.

Licorice is a plant! It was used as a medicine in China almost five thousand years ago.

GROW SOME FUN!

There are many interesting and unusual plants that you might enjoy planting. If you look through seed catalogs, you'll discover all sorts of incredible things to grow. Have you tried growing spaghetti squash? Purple potatoes? Lilac peppers? Dishrag gourds? Money plants? You can grow miniature pumpkins, white pumpkins, even 100-pound pumpkins. With so many neat plants to try, it's really hard to choose. Grow a few new things each season. Just follow the directions on the seed packet.

Here are some fun growing activities. Experiment a bit in your garden and come up with your own ideas. Keep track of your projects in your Garden Diary (page 96).

MATERIALS

Fresh plot of soil

Seeds, such as radish, grass, or birdseed

Pencil

Write your name in tiny green plants.

Use a pencil to dig narrow furrows in the soil in the shape of the letters of your name. Fill the furrows with seeds for tiny sprouts, such as radish, grass, or birdseed. Cover them lightly with soil. Keep it moist.

When the tiny plants emerge, your name will show up on the dark garden soil. Wouldn't it be fun to surprise someone special by planting their name?

Goofy Gourds

These are the most common gourd shapes. Their colors are usually green, orange, yellow, cream, and tan.

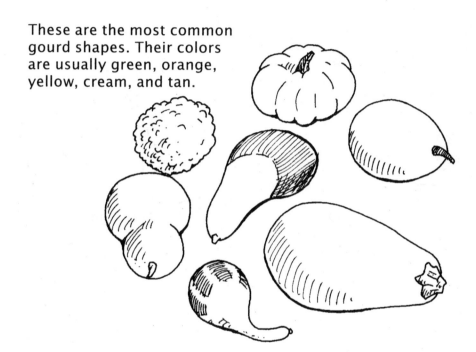

Gourds are fun to grow. They grow on long vines that will wrap themselves around fences or trellis supports. Grow them in a sunny spot, following the directions on the seed packet. Give the vines something to climb up on, and you'll be surprised with the colors and shapes of the gourds that grow. When the fall frost shrivels the vine's leaves, it's time to pick the gourds.

Gourds have been grown in North America for a long time. Native Americans used hollowed-out gourds to carry water and to use as drinking cups and bowls.

MATERIALS

Gourds of your choice
Paring knife (or electric drill with grown-up help)
Small hobby or coping saw, or serrated knife
Sandpaper
White glue
Brown shoe polish and soft cloth
Acrylic floor wax

Let your gourds dry and you can make all kinds of fun things. Use them as rattles, cut them to make birdhouses, use them as cups, bowls, scoops— or just leave them as they are for a pretty decoration in a basket of fall leaves.

Use a kitchen paring knife to cut holes in a dry gourd. First, use the knife point to work a small hole. Then, carve away at the hole to enlarge it. A grown-up can drill holes with an electric drill.

To make a cup or bowl, use a small saw or serrated knife to cut through the dry gourd. If the gourd cracks or breaks, repair it with white glue. Sand the rough edges with a small piece of sandpaper. Color the gourds with markers or rub on brown shoe polish with a soft cloth.

Save the dried seeds from inside the gourd for planting in the garden next spring.

To keep your gourds shiny and colorful, paint them with a coating of acrylic floor wax.

If you discover you have a real interest in gourds, you might want to write to the American Gourd Society, P.O. Box 274, Mt. Gilead, Ohio 43338. They can provide information and unusual seeds for gourd growers.

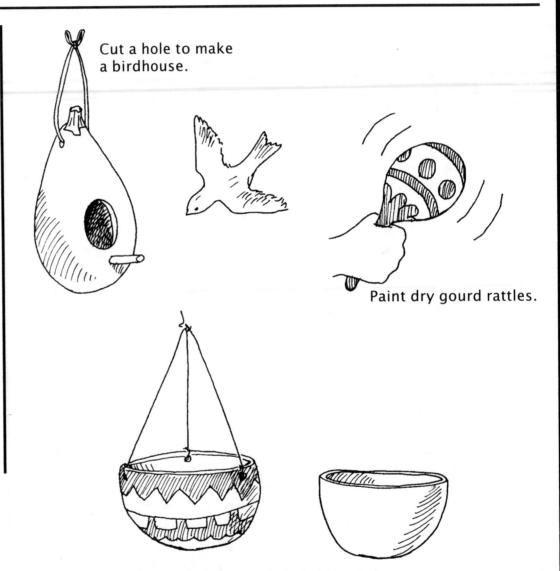

Cut a hole to make a birdhouse.

Paint dry gourd rattles.

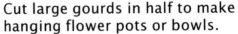

Cut large gourds in half to make hanging flower pots or bowls.

MATERIALS

6 forced bulbs
Flat dish or pretty bowl
Soil, or pretty marbles, stones, or gravel

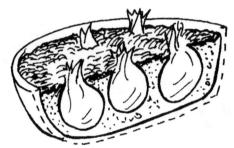

Plant bulbs in a dish of soil or gravel.

Use about 6 bulbs that have been treated for forcing indoors. This means that they were dug up in the fall, kept in a dark place, and then put in a cold place for several weeks. Chilling "fools" the bulb into thinking it's winter. When planted, the bulb begins growing just as it would in springtime. If you plan ahead, you can chill them yourself in a paper bag in the refrigerator, but you can also purchase them already chilled at a garden center.

One type of flowering plant grows each year from an onion-shaped root called a "bulb." Some names for these flowers are: narcissus, amaryllis, daffodil, lily, hyacinth, and crocus. There are others, but these are the most common. You can plant bulbs in a pot or dish and "force" them to grow, even in the winter!

Use a flat dish, or pretty bowl. Fill it with 2 or 3 inches of soil. The plant's food is already stored inside the bulb, so you could even hold the bulbs in place with pretty marbles or stones, if you like. Or use pretty gravel, such as the kind made for aquariums. Place the bulbs in the soil or gravel, and cover them, leaving the top tips uncovered. Plant the flat, root-growing end facing downward in the pot; the pointed end should be facing up.

Keep the soil or gravel wet, and place the pot in a cool but sunny window. In a few weeks, you will have fragrant blooms to enjoy, even if the snow is still on the ground outdoors!

When the bulbs are finished blooming, continue watering the pot, but let the leaves go dry (they hold food for the bulb). Later you can plant the bulbs in the garden.

Place the pot near a sunny window. In about 4 weeks, you'll have blooming flowers.

Crafty Crocus

Here's an easy gift idea everyone will love.

Flower bulbs were used as money long ago in Holland. Everyone wanted flower bulbs, and they were worth their weight in gold!

MATERIALS

3 to 6 crocus bulbs (pre-chilled in the refrigerator for 6 weeks)
Tuna can
½ cup colorful gravel or pebbles
8-inch fabric circle
Ribbon or colorful yarn

Put half of the gravel in the can, and carefully plant the crocus bulbs. Cover it with the rest of the gravel and fill the can with water to halfway up the sides of the bulbs. Put the can in a sunny spot and watch the bulbs grow.

Make a circle of fabric by tracing a dinner plate or pie pan. Wrap the can with the fabric and tie it with the ribbon or yarn. Whoever receives it will be amazed and delighted by the brightly colored little blooms.

MATERIALS

Venus flytrap plant
Large glass jar
Moss

 You can purchase a Venus flytrap plant, or the bulbs to grow them, from many garden supply stores. Mail-order companies, such as Gurney's, also sell them. (See Addresses, page 127.)

Find a large glass jar, about 1 gallon or larger. You might ask a restaurant for one of the large jars that they get bulk food in. Plant your Venus flytrap plant in a bed of moss in the glass jar. Keep it in sunlight, but not too hot or too cold. Let a glass of water sit out a day or so before using it to water the plant. The chlorine and chemicals that may harm such a sensitive plant will evaporate.

You can "feed" your plant dead houseflies, or tiny bits of hamburger. The leaves will snap shut, and later reopen when it is finished "eating."

Fascinating!

Yes, there really is a fantastic plant that eats its prey! The Venus flytrap plant has special wide leaves with jagged edges. The leaves are covered with special, sensitive "hair" that makes the leaves snap shut when a fly touches it. The leaves close quickly and trap the fly between them, where plant juices digest it.

Plant the Venus flytrap in a bed of moss in a large, glass jar.

Crazy Cucumber in a Bottle

Just wait till your friends see this magical feat! If you are growing cucumbers in your garden, you can grow one inside a bottle. Everyone will wonder how you got the cucumber through the tiny opening.

How did the cucumber get in the bottle?

It grew there!

MATERIALS

Clear plastic soda bottle
Cucumber vine from your garden
Cardboard

 Go into your garden, and find the end of a cucumber vine where a blossom has already "set" and a tiny cucumber is forming. Slip the end of the vine with the cucumber into the bottle. You may have to fold a piece of cardboard and set it on top of the bottle to shade the plant, because it may get too hot inside the bottle.

Check it every day because cucumbers grow quickly. When it's just right, break off the vine, and go find someone to amaze! You can also use squash or watermelon plants, and salad dressing bottles.

Here Kitty, Kitty!

MATERIALS

Catnip seeds or starter plants
Pots and potting soil
Woven fabric, such as denim, or a sock
Needle and thread

> *Does your kitty have fleas? Rub fresh pennyroyal, a herb, on her fur to keep them away.*

Stitch the fabric pieces together, leaving an opening.

After you fill it with catnip, stitch the pillow shut.

You can grow a plant that cats just love to nibble.

Your cat will be so excited.

Catnip seeds or starter plants can be purchased and grown in the garden or in pots near a window. Keep the cat away until the plant gets fully grown. Then snip fresh sprigs now and then and let the cat snack.

To make a toy for your cat, let the plant grow about two feet tall. Snip several sprigs and let them dry on a cookie sheet in a 150-degree oven. Strip the leaves from the branches and gently crush them with your fingers.

Cut shapes for the toy from firmly woven fabric, such as denim from old jeans. Cut two identical shapes, and place them right sides facing together. Stitch the shapes together around the outer edges, leaving a two-inch opening. Turn the fabric right side out and fill with the crushed catnip. Stitch the opening closed with a needle and a double length of thread. Make the stitches small and close together, so Kitty won't tear the toy open.

Another simple catnip toy can be made by filling a small sock with the dried catnip and tying the top together securely with yarn or heavy thread.

Watch a seed lift a penny!

MATERIALS

Bean seed
Egg carton
Soil
Penny
4 toothpicks

Plant a bean seed in an egg carton cup. Put a penny on top of the soil, right over the planted bean. Keep the soil moist and watch the bean lift the penny up with a push as it grows! Want to see how high it can lift the penny? Place four toothpicks around the penny to keep it from falling to the side, and watch the bean lift it an inch or so.

It's fun to have contests with friends, each planting a seed in the egg carton, and cheering on your own Super Seed. Who's bean seed can lift the penny first? Highest? How many pennies can a seed lift?

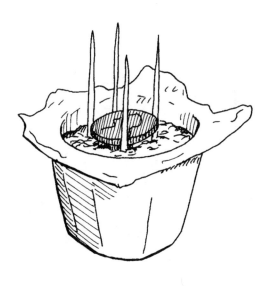
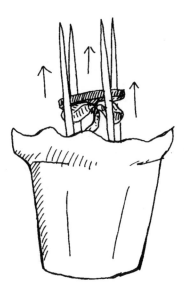

Watch each day to see how high the bean will push the penny.

MATERIALS

2 or 3 potatoes
Heavy-duty plastic lawn bag
Gravel
Soil
Knife

❀ Prepare the potatoes for planting by cutting them in pieces so that each piece has at least two "eyes," or buds, to sprout roots. Let the pieces dry out for a day or two.

Fold down the top of the bag a few times so that it will stay open. Put a layer of gravel on the bottom of the sack. Then, fill it with soil about 4 inches deep. Plant the potatoes and keep them watered. Place the sack in a box or laundry basket, so that you can move it to a sunny window or patio. Add more soil as the potatoes grow.

Pretty soon you'll have fresh new potatoes to enjoy. Boil them and add some chives from your herb pot.

How about a portable garden?

The ancient Inca people of South America were the first to grow potatoes. They ate them, but they also used them to cure aches and pains. Pieces of raw potato were pressed against the head to cure a headache. They rubbed slices of raw potato on their bodies to cure skin disease.

Incas invented "freeze-drying," too. They let potatoes freeze solid, then stamped them with their feet until they were a dry powder. That way they preserved them from rotting for months.

Small plants will sprout.

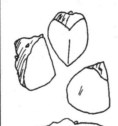

Cut up the potatoes. Make sure each section has at least 2 "eyes."

It's a garden in a bag.

Peanuts in a Pot

Yes, you can grow peanuts! They're not really nuts, but are plant relatives of "legumes" like lentils and beans. They are very interesting plants because the nut develops underground. For seed peanuts, be sure you are using nuts that have not been roasted. You can purchase them in some groceries, or order from a seed catalog.

Peanuts grow underground. It takes at least 4 months and lots of sunshine.

Peanuts will only grow in a warm sunny spot, with at least four months of growing season before frost. It's a good idea to start the plants in a pot indoors, then move the pot to the garden as soon as it warms up. Because they are so sensitive, plant the whole pot in the garden. That way the plant roots won't get disturbed.

Once the plant blooms, little shoots will grow out and down, going right into the soil, where the nuts will develop underground at the tips.

When the frost kills the plant in the fall, dig up the roots and nuts and lay them out to dry in the garden for a few days. Then, shake the dirt off and let the peanuts dry indoors in a cool, dry place.

Once they are dried, they look and feel more like the peanuts you are familiar with. Shell and roast the nuts on a cookie sheet in the oven at 350 degrees for about 20 minutes.

Grow a Bean Tent

MATERIALS

3 long stakes,
1 inch wide and 6 feet long

Heavy twine
Pole beans

You can make a secret hideaway for yourself right in the garden.

You can usually find stakes in garden departments; they're used to create plant supports. Push the ends of the stakes into the garden soil about six inches deep. Bring them together at the top, making a tripod. Tie the tops with the heavy twine. Plant "pole beans" at the base of each stake. Pole beans are plants with long vines and runners that will grow right up the stakes, creating a cozy private haven for a small gardener.

If you want to use more than three stakes and plant more beans, your hideaway will have even thicker walls. The beans will be good to eat, too!

MAKE & DO PROJECTS

What's a gardener to do when it's dark or too cold to go outside? Or if you don't have an outdoor garden spot? There are all sorts of projects and things you can make indoors. Here are some ideas you can enjoy when you can't work outdoors.

MATERIALS

Spiral notebook
Magazine cutouts
Paste
Clear plastic adhesive paper
Seed packets
String
Pen
Hole punch

All gardeners need diaries to keep track of their plants—when and where the seeds were planted, when they sprouted, and special things you did to make them grow better.

Turn an ordinary spiral notebook into a special garden book by pasting flower cutouts from colorful magazines on the cover. When the paste dries, lay a piece of clear plastic adhesive paper over it and press out all the wrinkles. Punch a hole in the cover and tie on a pen with a length of string.

Use the notebook as a diary or journal, writing down dates you planted seeds and the dates the plants came up. Keep track of what you've planted by drawing maps. Write down the date when vegetables were ready to pick.

Open up the seed packets you used and tape them to the page. Then, you can keep notes about the plants and how they grew. It will help you decide what to plant, or not to plant, next time.

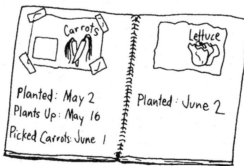

Plenty of Pots

You'll want to keep a box or bin full of pots to use for different planting projects. You can use almost anything to plant in, as long as it holds water and soil and has a large enough opening for the plant to spread out.

POT IDEAS

Old shoes
Cowboy boots
An upside-down hat or cap
Toy trucks
Wagons
Sand pail and buckets
Teapots
Coffee mugs
Plastic dishpans
Seashells
Baskets lined with plastic
Old purse
Yogurt cups
Cottage cheese containers
Glass jars
Coffee cans
Aluminum pans
from frozen foods

❀ Try one or all of the pot ideas listed. You can decorate the outside any way you like: cover your pot with colorful adhesive paper, dress it up with stickers, or try brightly colored spray paint. If you are using a pot that might not hold up to soil and water, such as a hat, put half of a plastic milk jug inside.

Here's a clever hanging planter made from a plastic tub. Save tubs from margarine, whipped topping, ice cream, whatever you find. Punch three holes in the top rim. Using a hole punch or a large nail, make the holes the same distance apart from one another around the rim. String the pot with three equal lengths of cord. Knot the three cords together at the top so it will hang from a hook.

Use your imagination to think of other unusual ways to pot your plants.

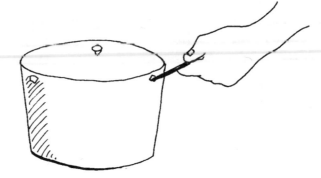

Punch holes around the rim with a nail.

Add cords and hang it up.

You don't have to buy seeds to get a garden started. Just save the seeds from things you eat at dinner. Search the kitchen and you'll find many different seeds. Look for avocado pits, popcorn, garlic, cucumber and squash seeds, potatoes, orange and grapefruit seeds, melon seeds, lentils, and beans.

Avocado

Save a pit, wash it, and poke three or four toothpicks in the sides. If the pit is too hard, use a small nail to work a hole in it for the toothpick. Let it hang down from the top of a glass into enough water to cover the lower half of the pit. Be sure you have it right-side up. For avocado pits, that means the small, pointed end should be up; the flat end with a tiny flat spot should be down in the water.

Let it sit in the water for a few weeks. Roots will grow from the bottom, and the top will split apart to let a green stem grow up. When the green stem is about 6 inches tall, trim it back to about 3 inches. This will make the plant grow other shoots out so it won't be tall and spindly.

When the avocado plant has a good root growth, plant it in a pot of soil, with half of the pit showing above the soil. Keep it moist, in a sunny spot.

Make sure the pointed end is up.

Sweet Potato

 Grow a sweet potato vine by starting the potato in a glass of water. Set the potato in the glass or jar of water so that at least ⅓ of it is under the water. Use toothpicks to suspend it from the rim of the glass. Place it on a windowsill and watch for the first sprouts.

Fresh sweet potatoes purchased in the fall will sprout more quickly than those that have been in storage for months. Most sweet potatoes are treated with a chemical that keeps them from sprouting in storage; this makes it harder for them to sprout in the winter or spring.

When your sweet potato has roots and leaves, it's time to plant it in a pot. Keep the soil moist, and put the plant in a sunny spot. The plant will grow long vines and lush green leaves. Clip it off now and then to make the plant create more leaves and less vine.

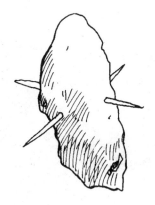

Pineapple

 Save the leafy top from a fresh pineapple. Be sure it has some of the core left on the leaf section. Let it sit a few days to dry out, so the bottom won't rot. Then plant it in a pot of moist soil. Firm the soil up around the core so it is covered. Water it a little every day to keep the soil moist. Let it sit in a sunny spot.

In a few weeks, you'll begin to see long flat green leaves sprout from the top. Keep watering and caring for the plant, and someday it may bear a tiny pineapple fruit for you to pick.

Plant it in a pot, and someday a tiny pineapple may grow.

Cut off the top.

Garlic

If you're an impatient gardener and can't wait to see things get growing, try garlic. It grows quickly, and will amaze you. Use a clove (a section) of fresh garlic. Poke three or four toothpicks into it, and balance it from the rim of a jar full of water. Be sure the flat end of the garlic is in the water. It's the end that was attached to the stem. Let it sit in a windowsill, and it will grow within days.

When the clove grows lots of healthy roots and a few green sprouts, pot it in a container of soil and keep it in a sunny spot until you can transplant it in your garden. It grows easily, and the odor it gives off keeps certain bugs away from other plants.

Make sure the flat end of the garlic is in the water.

Garlic Braid

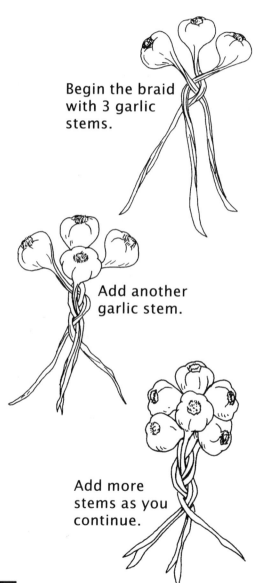

Begin the braid with 3 garlic stems.

Add another garlic stem.

Add more stems as you continue.

When the tops turn yellow, your garlic is ready to harvest. Here's a good way to store it. Make a braid and hang it from a hook or nail in the kitchen. Give garlic braids as gifts, or sell them.

Use fresh garlic right from the garden because its leaves are flexible enough to braid. Rinse the soil off the plants. Begin with three heads and arrange them together to start a braid. Braid the leaves tightly once or twice, then add a fourth head of garlic over the center one. Add its leaves with one of the others and braid twice more. Add more heads as you go, adding two heads now and then instead of one. Repeat until it's as long as you want, or until you run out of garlic. Tie the ends together with a piece of twine.

Hang it in a dry place so that the garlic will dry out. That way it will last a long time. When you want to use some in cooking, break off a head from the braid.

Knot the ends with twine.

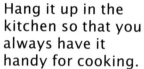

Hang it up in the kitchen so that you always have it handy for cooking.

The people who built the ancient Egyptian pyramids were fed garlic to make them stronger so they could work harder.

Dish Garden

Anyone can plant a dish garden—it's an easy way to watch things grow.

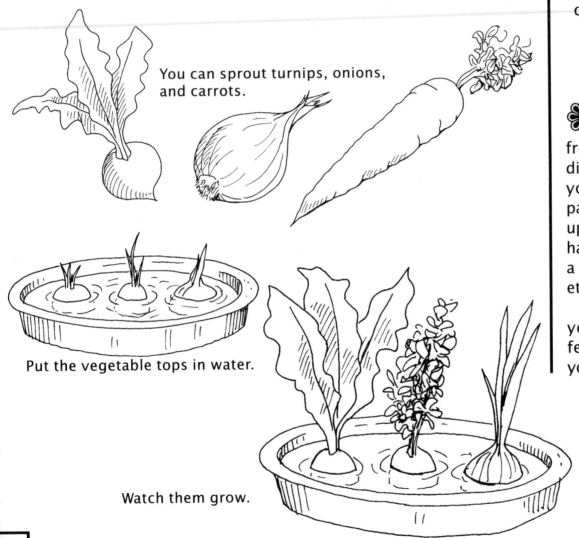

You can sprout turnips, onions, and carrots.

Put the vegetable tops in water.

Watch them grow.

MATERIALS

Vegetable tops:
carrot, onion, potato, turnip, beets, and celery
Flat dish
Water

❀ Find a flat dish, such as a pie pan. Place the tops from various vegetables in the dish; use leftovers from a meal you might have made. Fill the pan with water, and keep it filled up enough to cover the bottom half of the vegetable tops. Put in a windowsill and watch the vegetables begin to sprout.

Once things are growing well, you may want to transplant a few of the plants into pots or your garden.

Blooming Branches

Clip some branches from a tree or shrub.

Put them in water and they'll bloom.

 Wait until the end of winter, in February or March, when the branches have buds beginning to form. Cut off some branches that have buds forming on them. Between 12 and 18 inches long is a good length. Bring them indoors and put them in a large vase of water. Keep the water level filled, so that the branches have plenty to drink.

Keep the vase of branches in a cool place for a few days, so that the branches get used to the indoor temperatures. Then move them to a sunny area near a window, where they can leaf out and blossom.

If you don't have trees in your yard to clip branches from, ask a nursery to save some of their prunings for you. It's great to have new leaves and blossoms while snow still covers the ground outdoors!

Even in winter, a gardener can find something interesting to do with plants. If you have fruit trees in the yard, or shrubs that blossom in the spring, you can bring a few branches indoors and watch as they burst with leaves, and maybe even blossoms.

Topiary

MATERIALS

Wire coat hanger
2 or 3 small ivy plants
Pot
Potting soil
Pliers

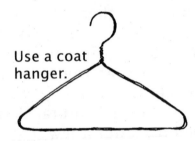

Use a coat hanger.

A topiary is a plant that has been trained or clipped into an interesting shape. Topiaries are made from dark green leafy plants because the shape shows up well.

Topiary gardens were popular in the long-ago days of the ancient Romans. Since that time, queens have designed them for their castles, and even Disneyland has an interesting display of characters formed by shrubbery.

You can make a clever topiary project to sit on a tabletop.

Root some ivy cuttings in a jar of water a few weeks before you're going to do this project. The ivy will be ready for planting by this time.

Untwist the coat hanger and shape it into something clever for your ivy to grow over. A heart is very easy, and so is a circle or cross. Now make the part that will hold your topiary up. Attach a second, straight piece of wire at the bottom of the special shape you just made by twisting it firmly. Push this part down into the pot of soil so that it sits securely.

Now plant the ivy in the pot. Keep it moist and in a sunny spot. As the ivy grows, gently guide it over the wire shape until it covers the whole thing.

Start some ivy sprouts.

Bend the hanger into a special shape and stick it into the soil.

Plant some ivy cuttings and train them to grow over the hanger.

Sprout a Silly Pet

Here's a clever way to make a creature that grows a "furry" coat.

Keep your animal moist.

MATERIALS

1 pound modeling clay
(the kind that doesn't harden, such as Plastilina)

Rye grass, chia, or alfalfa seeds*

Quart-size plastic bag with fastener

Paper towel

Spray bottle of water

*Don't use store-bought birdseed. It's been treated with chemicals to keep it from sprouting and doesn't sprout as quickly.

Use a large chunk of clay to create a creature—anything you like. Press seeds firmly into the clay wherever you want "fur" to grow. Be sure to use plenty of seeds; try to cover the clay. Make sure you press the seeds firmly into the clay so that they won't fall off. Spray your animal completely with water.

Wet the paper towel and fold it to fit the bag. Carefully place the pet in the bag on top of the paper towel. Fasten the bag so that the moisture won't escape. Keep an eye on the pet and spray it every day. Continue spraying to keep the seeds damp. If the seeds begin to get moldy, open the bag for a day or two to let them dry out.

When your beast begins to sprout "fur," take it out and display it in a sunny windowsill.

Watch the fur sprout all over.

MATERIALS

Small shrub or tree seedling: juniper, pine, fir, or cypress

Tray, dish, or pan
Scissors
Dinner fork
Potting soil

Bonsai is a Japanese art form made by trimming a tree so it stays small, and can be enjoyed indoors in a tray. The Chinese began clipping and training bonsai trees 2,000 years ago. The Japanese developed it further. In Japan, some bonsai trees are handed down from one generation to the next. Maybe you can grow a bonsai tree to pass on to your own children someday.

 The best plants to use are juniper shrubs, in 1-gallon pots from a nursery. You can also use small fruit trees or flowering shrubs.

Use scissors to cut off the branches close to the trunk. Don't let chopped-off stumps from branches stick out. Keep the trunk smooth. You want it to look like a tiny replica of a full-grown tree.

Prepare the pot. You can use a pretty pot, such as a flat casserole-type dish. Look at yard sales or thrift shops. Spread a layer of gravel, and then fill the pot with potting soil.

Gently take the plant out of its container and use the fork to carefully pull away some of the dirt around the roots. You'll need to use the scissors to trim off about 1/3 of the roots. This will help keep the tree small.

Plant it in the pot and add pretty rocks, a seashell, or moss to make it look even more artful and elegant.

Water it regularly when the soil dries out. Trim the branches as the tree grows. Be sure it gets plenty of light near a window. Because it is kept indoors in a small pot, it won't grow very fast.

Keep trimming your bonsai in the shape of a miniature tree.

Grow an Easter Basket

 Plan this about 10 days ahead of Easter.

Tear the bag apart at the seam and lay it inside the basket, letting some spread over the sides all around. Add potting soil to the basket so that it's about two-thirds full. Use the scissors to trim away some of the plastic bag that is sticking out. Press a few handfuls of seed into the soil, and pat it firmly.

Place the basket in a sunny spot. Keep it damp by spraying it with water when necessary.

When the grass is ready, tuck the plastic bag so that it doesn't show. Wrap colorful ribbons around the basket handle to decorate it. Fill it with colorful eggs.

You can also grow an Easter basket in a plastic berry basket lined with aluminum foil. Prepare the basket ahead of time by cutting strips of colored construction paper and weaving in-and-out to cover the basket.

MATERIALS

Basket
Lawn seed, or soft wheat berries (sold in the health-food section of the grocery store)
Potting soil
Plastic bag
Spray bottle filled with water

Line the basket with plastic, fill it with soil, and plant grass seeds.

In 2 weeks, it will be ready to decorate and hide Easter eggs in.

Make a Flower Press

MATERIALS

2 pieces heavy cardboard
(from a box)

Masking tape or
colorful plastic tape

X-acto knife

2 ribbons, each a yard long

Paper towels

Heavy books

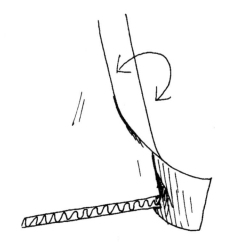

Fold tape over to cover the
cardboard edges.

Pressed flowers should be gathered early in the morning, when the dew has dried but while the blossoms are still fresh. You can press them to save for craft projects next winter. They're nice to glue to greeting cards, bookmarks, or holiday placemats.

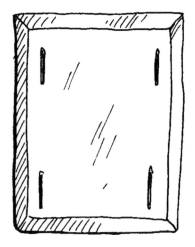
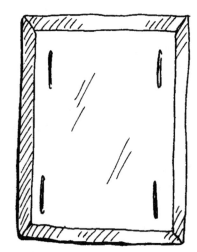

Cut 4 slits in both cardboard pieces.

Cover the edges of the cardboard with tape to make it look nice and neat. Cut four slits in the corners of both pieces of cardboard with the X-acto knife. Make them wide enough for the ribbon to slide through. Thread the ribbon through the slits.

Lay a few layers of paper towels between the cardboard sections. As you gather the fresh flowers, position them carefully between the paper towels. Tie the ribbons to close the press. When you get home, stack some heavy books on top of the flower press to help flatten the blossoms. Check the flowers every few days. It will take a few weeks for them to dry completely, depending on the flowers' thickness.

Do you know any of these old-fashioned rhymes? You can say them as you pluck flower petals, to find out what your future holds!

Does your sweetheart love you? "He loves me, he loves me not," or: "She loves me, she loves me not."

When will you marry? "This year, next year, sometime, never."

Where will you live? "Big house, little house, pigsty, barn."

What will you wear? "Silk, satin, calico, rags."

What will you be? "Rich, poor, beggar, thief, doctor, lawyer, Indian chief."

Lay the flowers between the paper towels inside your press.

Tie the press closed with the ribbons.

Frame a Leaf

MATERIALS

Pretty leaves (ferns are perfect)

Stiff clear plastic sheets
(sheet protectors in the
office supply or photography
department)

Heavy tape
(silver or bright colors)

Glue

Select a pretty leaf. Make sure that it's not torn and that it is as flat as possible. Press the leaf flat. Use your Flower Press (page 110).

Lay the leaf between the plastic sheets. Trim them to size if necessary; you don't want too large an area around the leaf. Use a drop of glue to hold the leaf in place. Tape the edges of the plastic together, folding half the tape over to cover the back piece of plastic.

Use your framed leaf as a bookmark. You can also punch a hole in it and hang it from a delicate cord or ribbon; it makes a beautiful ornament.

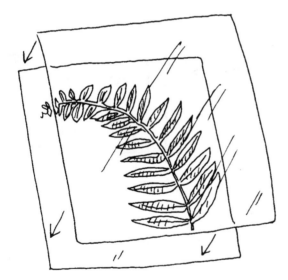

Place the leaf between 2 sheets of plastic.

Fold tape around the edges.

You can use garden materials to make dolls. Pioneer children made their own dolls from materials they found around the house or farm. You can make some of these folk dolls to create a collection, or share with your friends.

Cornhusk Doll

Fold the cornhusks, and tie them with string to make a head.

Fold and tie the ends of another husk to make arms.

Put the arms under the head, and tie them in place.

Draw a face with markers. Add cornsilk or moss hair.

You can make a doll wearing pants, too.

MATERIALS

Cornhusks
Heavy string
Scissors
Permanent markers
Glue

 Stack several large husks and fold them in the center. Tie them with string near the fold to make a head. Fold some smaller husks lengthwise into the arm section, and tie the ends with string. Slide it up inside the body and tie string around the middle to make a waist. Trim the bottom to make a skirt.

For a doll with legs, divide the body section into two parts and tie the ankles with string. Glue on corn silk or moss for hair.

MATERIALS

Lima bean
Two 1-by-2-inch
cotton fabric scraps
Needle and thread
Craft glue
Fine-tipped permanent marker

Use 1 large
lima bean.

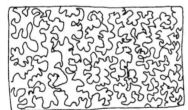

Cut 2 fabric rectangles.

Bean Doll

You need one bean for each doll. Cut two fabric rectangles, each 1 by 2 inches. Wrap one around the bean head and glue it in place like a scarf. Gather the fabric for the skirt and make stitches along one of its long edges. Put the head inside the skirt, neck facing up. Pull up the thread in the gathers around the neck and stitch tightly all around, stitching through the neck. Turn the doll right side out.

Draw on a tiny face if you wish. Fine-tipped permanent markers work best. Make an entire lima bean family.

Glue 1 rectangle
on the bean like
a scarf.

Stitch along
1 edge of the
second piece
of fabric.

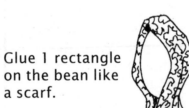

Gather up the
fabric like a
skirt. Place the
bean, upside
down, inside
the skirt. Pull
the gathers
tightly.

Draw a face.

Grow Some Mold

That's right! Mold is a plant, too. You can grow some on a piece of bread.

Moisten half a slice of bread with water, and put it in a closed glass jar.

Greenish mold plants will grow.

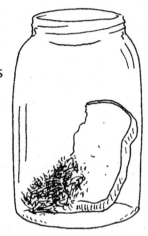

MATERIALS

White bread
Jar with lid
Water
Magnifying lens

Molds, fungi, and mushrooms are related. They grow by living on something else: tree bark, rotted leaves, or even bread. They grow from spores, not seeds.

Wet a piece of fresh white bread. Put it in the jar, fasten the lid, and put it in a cupboard for a few days. You'll notice the soft, feathery mold plants begin to grow right away.

Find an old orange that has green mold on it. Keep it in a jar in a dark warm place. In a few days, the mold will grow and look like fluffy spider webs.

Use a magnifying lens to look closely at the little stems with tiny black knobs on them. These are spore cases. Each case holds thousands of spores. When the mold ripens, the spore cases break open and the spores travel through the air to begin new mold plants. The air we breathe is filled with mold spores, but we can't see or smell them.

It's fun to experiment with mold plants. Compare light and dark, or warm and cold growing conditions. Also, try growing mold in a dry or moist place. You'll discover how they grow best.

Tiny cases release spores that travel through the air and create new mold plants.

Awesome Algae

MATERIALS

Pond water
Glass jar
Magnifying lens or microscope

To watch algae grow, collect some pond water in a jar. Let it sit in a warm, sunny spot (the algae needs sun, just like other plants). Watch the water get greener as the tiny plants grow. Use a magnifying lens or microscope to see the tiny water plants better.

*A*lgae—that slimy, greenish stuff in pond water—is a plant! It's one of the smallest, simplest plants on Earth, and you can grow some in a jar.

Algae contains the special substance *chlorophyll*. It makes plants green, and it makes it possible for the plant to make food from sunlight.

Algae grows in salt water or fresh water. Many water animals eat algae, but so do people! Did you know that *carrageen*, a salt-water algae, is used to make your ice cream creamy smooth? You bet!

Put the jar of water in the sunlight because algae needs light to grow.

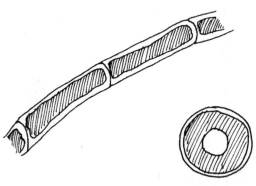

Algae plants look like this when you see them through a microscope.

Yeast is a plant, too. It doesn't have chlorophyll, so it won't have a green color like leafy plants do. A microscope will help when you want to view the tiny plants. They look like little oval cells with buds on them.

Mix the water, sugar, and yeast together in a covered jar.

This is what yeast plants look like through a microscope.

MATERIALS

⅔ cup warm water
5 teaspoons sugar
1 teaspoon dry yeast
Jar with lid
Microscope

Mix the water, sugar, and yeast together in a jar. Cover it with a lid. Look at a sample with your microscope. Let it sit a few minutes. What happens? Leave it in a warm place for two days. Now what do you see? Yeast plants grow by bubbling. As they multiply, they let off carbon dioxide gas which makes frothy bubbles. It's this same action from yeast that makes bread rise during baking.

Yeast plants need food, like all plants. They grow very quickly with the help of sugar.

Many gardeners sell what they grow. When vegetables and flowers are ready to pick, fill a basket with your best items and visit your neighbors. They may want to buy the luscious vegetables and fragrant flowers when they see how nice they are. They might also want to place orders for future pickings, too.

Many towns have a Farmers' Market, where gardeners sell their fruits, vegetables, herbs, flowers, and crafts. Check this out—you may be able to sell your items, too.

Plan ahead and dry flowers and herbs to sell at Thanksgiving and Christmas time. You can use your garden crops to create holiday wreaths, potpourri, jars of dried parsley with calico covers, sprigs of dried lavender to scent a room, swags of braided garlic—all for sale to eager customers.

Garden Sounds

Make a tape recording of the sounds in your garden. Listen to the birds, bees, crickets, and frogs. Next winter you'll be able to turn it on, close your eyes, and remember those warm summer days.

Can you hear plants grow? Some people say that you can hear a field of corn as it grows! If you can borrow a stethoscope, you can try to hear the "heartbeat" of a big tree. The stethoscope can pick up the sound of the sap as it flows up the tree.

Scientists have discovered that certain sounds cause pores in plant leaves to open—causing stronger growth. Maybe chirping birds' songs help plants grow better! Let those crickets sing!

THINK AHEAD!

Part of gardening is looking to the future, not just thinking about this year's harvest but about next year's crop, too. For thousands of years, gardeners have saved seeds from their best plants for the next crop. Such seeds are called "heirloom" seeds, since they are handed down from generation to generation. You can save seeds from your best plants, and plant them the following year. Continue saving and planting, and you'll have "heirloom" seeds to pass along, too!

Save Some Seeds

Store dry seeds in labeled envelopes in a shoebox.
Next spring you'll be able to plant them!

MATERIALS

Seeds from your own plants
Cookie sheet
Envelopes
Shoebox
Marker

If you plan ahead, you can save seeds for next year's planting.

Tomato, pea, bean, cucumber, watermelon, squash, and potatoes can be replanted from seeds you've saved. You can save flower seeds, such as marigolds, zinnias, alyssum, snapdragons, poppies, and sunflowers, too.

Only save seeds from the very best plants. You don't want to grow puny plants, so don't use seed from plants that aren't strong and healthy. People who grow prize-winning pumpkins only save seeds from their largest pumpkins, choosing the biggest each year.

Pick the seeds out of the fruit or vegetable. Rinse them with water, and let them dry on a cookie sheet.

Label some envelopes to store the seeds in. Write what kind of seeds they are, what year you grew them, and any other information you think is important. It's easy to forget which seed is which over the winter.

File them in a shoebox. Be careful to store them in a cool, dry location; if the seeds get damp, they might sprout before you want them to.

Some seeds can't be saved. They come from "hybrid" plants. Hybrid plants have been created by combining plants, and their seeds won't grow plants identical to the parent plant.

It's important to save seeds because many old types of plants are lost when no one saves and plants the seeds. If people don't save the seeds, these plants will soon become extinct. Our plant heritage will be lost.

Grow Some History

If you visit a historical site, ask the guide for permission to take a seed home with you. You can plant a relative of a tree or flower that grew at a Civil War battlefield, on the Oregon Trail, or at a Spanish Mission.

Your yard will have a lot of interesting plants, and you'll have souvenirs to remember your trips with.

Did you know that the United States has a National Herb Garden and a National Bonsai Collection? Both are planted in the National Arboretum, in Washington, D.C. It is America's "Living Museum" in the Nation's Capital. If you visit, you can see special gardens like the Early American Garden, with plants the colonists grew, and the American Indian Garden, with wild plants the Native Americans gathered.

Perhaps there is a special garden museum, botanical garden, or arboretum near your home. They will not only have beautiful plantings for you to see, but they often sell seeds and small plants that you can take home for your own garden.

Long ago, people carried sprigs of certain plants because they thought they were magical. They thought plants would keep dragons away and prevent "elf-sickness."

Trees

Trees are the biggest, grandest green plants of all! We need them to clean the air we breathe. Plant one on a birthday or anniversary, and have someone take a photo of you standing next to it every year. You'll both be growing older and taller!

Choose the kind of tree best for your yard and climate. You can read about different trees in garden catalogs and see pictures of how they will look when they're fully grown. Select the best spot in your yard to plant the tree. It should not be too close to a building, under a power line, or in the shadow of another tree.

Dig a hole at least twice as wide as the tree's root ball and almost that deep. Set the tree in the center of the hole. Crumble the soil back into the hole, adding compost if you have it. Fill the soil in around the tree, sprinkling with water to settle. Add a layer of mulch around the newly planted tree. Keep the tree well-watered between rains.

FUTURE GARDENS

Our ancestors could not survive without plants. Their food came from plants, their clothing was made from plant fibers, or the skin of animals that ate plants. Their homes were made with wood from trees, branches, and grasses.

Life on earth hasn't changed that much over the centuries. We use cotton, linen (from flax), and ramie for clothing; live in houses of wood; eat fruits and vegetables; and depend on plants to clear the air we breathe. Even the paper this book is printed on came from the plant world.

But plants have much more to give us. Medicines also come from plants. Many of today's medicines are "copies" of chemicals from plants. For example, aspirin came from the spirea plant. Native Americans used the plant as a medicine, but it upset the stomach. A German scientist studied the plant to create the medicine we use today for headaches and fever. Scientists today are discovering new medicines from plants, such as the yew tree, that can cure some cancers. There may be many more to be discovered in the future!

Growing a garden and learning about plants can be more than a hobby. You may decide to make a career of growing or studying them. How about traveling to remote jungles searching for exotic plants to create medicines from? Maybe you'd be happy working with an archaeologist, studying ancient seeds and plant remains for clues to the past. You may decide to work at restoring the forests by starting trees in giant greenhouses. Scientists are working to create unusual blends of plant and animal cells right now.

You might be one of the people who chooses to make a career in the plant world. There's a lot of excitement to look forward to once you begin gardening—indoors or out!

RESOURCES

You can buy nearly all your garden supplies by mail-order. Write to these addresses for their catalogs, and you can study the pictures, read information about many plants, and learn more about gardening.

Addresses

W. Atlee Burpee & Company
300 Park Avenue
Warminster, PA 18974

Henry Field's Seed & Nursery
   Company
415 North Burnett
Shenandoah, IA 51602
(seeds, helpful insects)

Gurney's Seed & Nursery
   Company
110 Capital Street
Yankton, SD 57079
(vegetables, herbs, Venus
   flytraps, helpful insects)

Native Seeds/SEARCH
2509 N. Campbell Avenue, #325
Tucson, AZ 85719
(seed-saving organization)

Nichols Garden Nursery
1190 North Pacific Highway
Albany, OR 97321-4580
(herbs, rare seeds, paper tea bags)

Park Seed Company
Cokesbury Road
Greenwood, SC 29647-0001

Seeds Blum
Idaho City Stage
Boise, ID 83706
(heirloom vegetable seeds,
    interesting catalog, $3.00)

Seeds of Change
PO Box 15700
Santa Fe, NM 87506-5700
(heirloom seeds)

Spring Hill Nurserie
110 West Elm Street
Tipp City, OH 45371
(roses, bulbs)

Stokes Seeds, Inc.
Box 548
Buffalo, NY 14240-0548

Books & Magazines

Andrews, Jonathan. *The Country Diary Book of Creating a Wild Flower Garden.* New York: Henry Holt and Company, 1987.

Burke, Ken, ed. *How to Attract Birds.* San Ramon, Calif.: Ortho Books, 1983.

Buske, Terry, ed. *Llewellyn's Lunar Organic Gardener.* St. Paul, Minn.: Llewellyn Publications, 1992.

Child's First Library of Learning: Insect World. Alexandria, Va.: Time-Life Books, 1988.

Coon, Nelson. *Using Wayside Plants.* New York: Hearthside Press, 1960.

Cox, Jeff. *Landscaping with Nature.* Emmaus, Penn.: Rodale Press, 1991.

Gallup, Barbara, and Deborah Reich. *The Complete Book of Topiary.* New York: Workman Publishing, 1987.

Lathrop, Norma Jean. *Herbs: How to Select, Grow and Enjoy.* Los Angeles: HPBooks, 1981.

Newmann, Erik A. *A Guide to the Major Gardens and Collections: The U.S. National Arboretum.* Washington, D.C.: National Capital Area Federation of Garden Clubs, 1989.

Niethammer, Carolyn. *American Indian Food and Lore.* New York: Collier Books, 1974.

Organic Gardening Magazine. Minor, Penn.: Rodale Press.

Rapp, Lynn, and Joe Rapp. *Grow with Your Plants.* New York: Bantam Books, 1976.

Sunset Guide to Organic Gardening. Menlo Park, Calif.: Sunset Books, 1973.

Viola, Herman, and Carolyn Margolis. *Seeds of Change.* Washington, D.C.: Smithsonian Institution, 1991.

Wernert, Susan J., ed. *North American Wildlife.* Pleasantville, New York: Reader's Digest Books, 1982.

Yee, Min S., ed. *Houseplants.* Mt. Vernon, Va.: American Horticultural Society, 1980.

Index of Plants

M

marigolds, 20, 52
marjoram, 75, 79
milkweed, 52
mint, 64, 67, 69, 72, 79
mold, 115
mums, 26
mung beans, 60

N

narcissus, 85
nasturtiums, 20, 52, 57, 62, 63

O

onions, 61, 66, 76, 104
oregano, 66, 69, 75

P

pansies, 62
parsley, 57, 67, 69, 75
peanuts, 93
peonies, 26
peppermint, 71

philodendrons, 26
pigweed, 41
pine, 108
pineapples, 101
pinecones, 21
poison ivy and oak, 61
pokeweed, 42
potatoes, 66, 75, 92, 104
pumpkins, 81

Q

quack grass, 41

R

radishes, 20, 57, 82
rosemary, 66, 79
roses, 57, 62, 64, 79
rye grass, 107

S

sage, 26, 57, 67, 69, 77
snapdragons, 20
soft wheat berries, 109
spearmint, 71
spices, 70

squash, 20, 66
sunflowers, 20, 49
sweet potatoes, 100

T

tomatoes, 57, 66, 73
topiary, 106
trees, 105, 125
turnip, 66, 104

V

Venus flytrap, 88
violets, 52, 62, 64
Virginia Creeper vines, 49

W

watermelons, 20
weeds, 21, 41

Y

yeast, 117

Z

zinnias, 20, 52
zucchini, 62, 76

More Books by Laurie Carlson from Chicago Review Press

Huzzah Means Hooray
Activities from the Days of Damsels, Jesters, and Blackbirds in a Pie

Kids can re-create a long-ago world of kings, castles, jousts, jesters, magic fairies, and Robin Hood—all they need are their imaginations and materials they can find at home.

ages 3–9
ISBN 1-55652-227-4
184 pages, paper, $12.95

Kids Camp!
Activities for the Backyard or Wilderness

with Judith Dammel

Camping is more fun and educational than ever before with this book, which shows kids how to construct a tarp tent, make jean daypacks, tie knots, press flowers, go on scavenger hunts, tell time from a sun clock, and even make the ultimate lunch: hot dogs and s'mores cooked in a solar oven, washed down with a cup of wilderness punch.

ages 4–12
ISBN 1-55652-237-1
184 pages, paper, $12.95

More Than Moccasins
A Kid's Activity Guide to Traditional North American Indian Life

Kids will discover traditions and skills handed down from the people who first settled this continent, including how to plant a garden, make useful pottery, and communicate through Navajo code talkers.

"As an educator who works with Indian children I highly recommend [More Than Moccasins] for all kids and teachers...I learned things about our Indian world I did not know."

—Bonnie Jo Hunt
Wicahpi Win (Star Woman)
Standing Rock Lakota

ages 3–9
ISBN 1-55652-213-4
200 pages, paper, $12.95

Other Kid's Activity Books from Chicago Review Press

Big Book of Fun
Creative Learning Activities for Home & School, Ages 4–12
Carolyn Buhai Haas
Illustrated by Jane Bennett Phillips
Includes more than 200 projects and activities—from indoor-outdoor games and nature crafts to holiday ideas, cooking fun, and much more.
ISBN 1-55652-020-4
280 pages, paper, $11.95

Frank Lloyd Wright for Kids
Kathleen Thorne-Thomsen
A thorough biography is followed by stimulating projects that enable kids to grasp the ideas underlying Wright's work—and have fun in the process.
ages 8 and up
ISBN 1-55652-207-X
144 pages, paper, $14.95

Happy Birthday, Grandma Moses
Activities for Special Days Throughout the Year
Clare Bonfanti Braham and Maria Bonfanti Esche
Illustrations by Mary Jones
The significance of 100 different celebratory days is thoroughly explained as 200 related activities pay charming, educational tribute to the holidays, history, and accomplishments of many cultures and many people.
ages 3–9
ISBN 1-55652-226-6
304 pages, paper, $14.95

Look at Me
Creative Learning Activities for Babies and Toddlers
Carolyn Buhai Haas
Illustrated by Jane Bennett Phillips
Activities for babies and toddlers that inspire creativity and learning through play.
ISBN 1-55652-021-2
228 pages, paper, $11.95

Messy Activities and More
Virginia K. Morin
Illustrated by David Sokoloff
Foreword by Ann M. Jernberg
Encourages adults and children to have fun making a mess with more than 160 interactive games and projects.
ages 3–10
ISBN 1-55652-173-1
144 pages, paper, $9.95

My Own Fun
Creative Learning Activities for Home and School
Carolyn Buhai Haas and Anita Cross Friedman
More than 160 creative learning projects and activities for elementary-school children.
ages 7–12
ISBN 1-55652-093-X
194 pages, paper, $9.95

These books are available through your local bookstore or directly from Independent Publishers Group, 814 N. Franklin Street, Chicago, Illinois, 60610, 1-800-888-4741.
Visa and MasterCard accepted.